THE
GENTLEMAN'S
WARDROBE

THE GENTLEMAN'S WARDROBE

VINTAGE-STYLE PROJECTS FOR THE MODERN MAN

VANESSA MOONCIE

First published 2017 by
Guild of Master Craftsman Publications Ltd
Castle Place, 166 High Street, Lewes,
East Sussex BN7 1XU

Text © Vanessa Mooncie, 2017
Copyright in the Work © GMC Publications Ltd, 2017

ISBN 978 1 86108 747 8

While every effort has been made to obtain permission from
the copyright holders for all material used in this book, the
publishers will be pleased to hear from anyone who has not
been appropriately acknowledged and to make the
correction in future reprints.

The publishers and author can accept no legal responsibility
for any consequences arising from the application of
information, advice or instructions given in this publication.

A catalogue record for this book is available from the
British Library.

Publisher: Jonathan Bailey
Production Manager: Jim Bulley
Senior Project Editor: Wendy McAngus
Editor: Nicola Hodgson
Managing Art Editor: Gilda Pacitti
Art Editor: Rebecca Mothersole
Photographers: Chris Gloag and Richard Boll
Illustrations by Vanessa Mooncie

Colour origination by GMC Reprographics
Printed and bound in China

CONTENTS

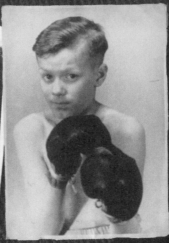

Introduction

I often look back at old black and white photographs of my grandparents, their families and friends (*above*), looking immaculate in shirts and ties, smart trousers, jackets and overcoats, and almost always accessorised with a trilby and gloves. Even on days out at the seaside, the ladies looked so pretty in their summer dresses and cloche hats or silk scarves, and the gentlemen dapper with their short-sleeved shirts, slicked-back hair and handkerchief neatly folded in their pocket or knotted on their head. Although they had little money to spend on their wardrobe, they always took great care over their appearance.

The family photos, along with a cravat and a 'dickie-bow' tie that belonged to my Great Uncle Albert, inspired me to design a collection of garments and accessories for men that reflected the attention they paid to their image all those years ago. *The Gentleman's Wardrobe* is a collection of sewing patterns for clothing and accessories to make for the discerning chap, all explained with easy-to-follow, illustrated step-by-step instructions.

The 14 projects range from uncomplicated pieces, such as a pair of felt slippers and a bow tie, to more complex patterns, including a tailored jacket and messenger bag. The techniques section at the back of the book will equip you with all you need to know to create each item.

The fabrics and fastenings you choose will influence how your finished project will look. For example, a traditional tweed or suiting fabric will give the jacket a vintage appearance, whereas making it in denim, or using a bold print, will produce a very different style. Whatever you use, these handmade items will furnish your wardrobe and will be a unique expression of yourself.

Vanessa Mooncie

Cravat, page 128

Opposite:
DRESSING GOWN Page № 96

This page: **WAISTCOAT** Page № 46

Right: **SHIRT** Page № 28

Below: **WALLET** Page № 118

WAISTCOAT Page № 46
TROUSERS Page № 54

Opposite: **SUMMER SHIRT** Page №38
This page: **JACKET** Page №66

This page: **BOW TIE** Page № *124*
Opposite, top: **CRAVAT** Page № *128*
Opposite, below: **BOW TIE** Page № *124*

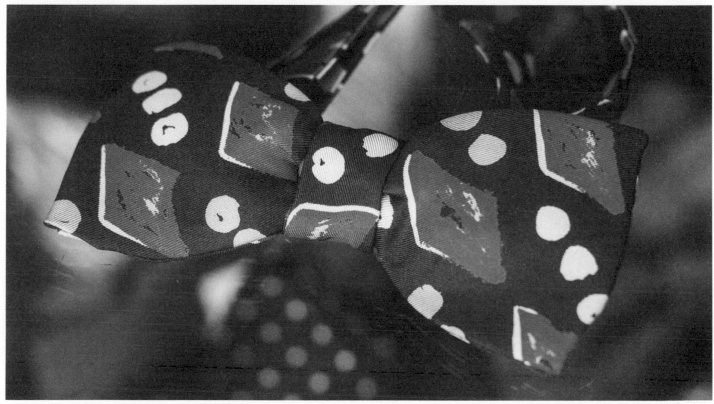

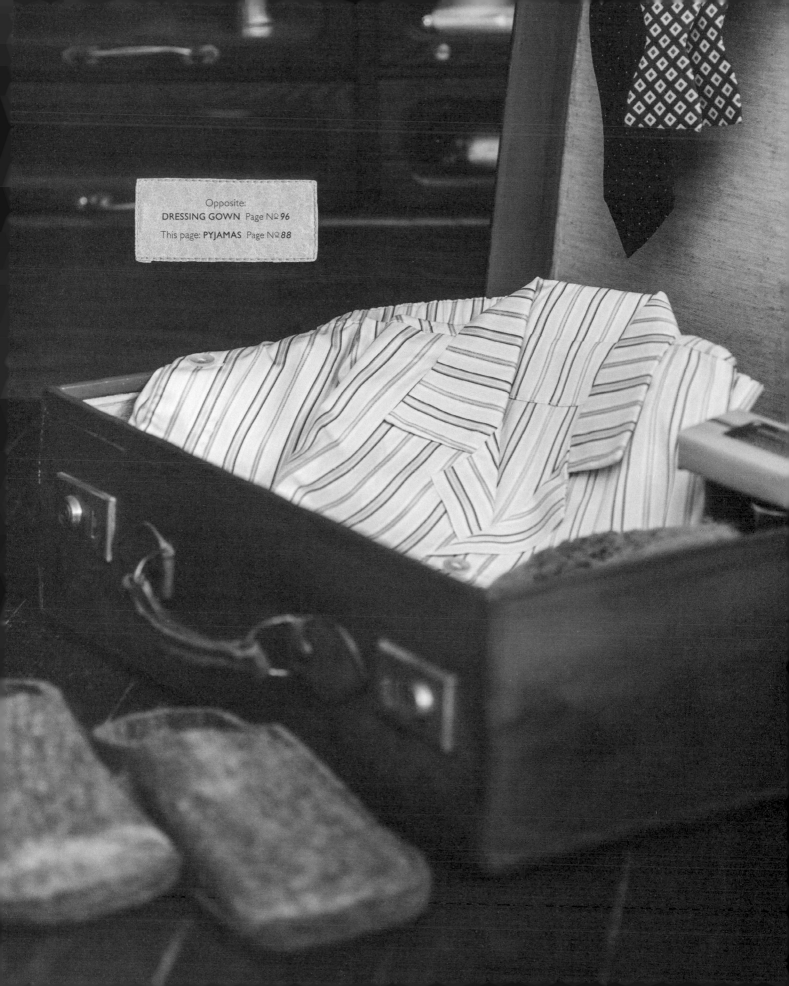

Opposite:
DRESSING GOWN Page №*96*

This page: **PYJAMAS** Page №*88*

Opposite: **FLAT CAP** Page № *132*
This page: **WAISTCOAT** Page № *46*

Opposite:
MESSENGER BAG Page № 110

This page: SHIRT Page № 28

Opposite: **BOXER SHORTS** Page № *80*

This page: **SLIPPERS** Page № *104*

Daywear

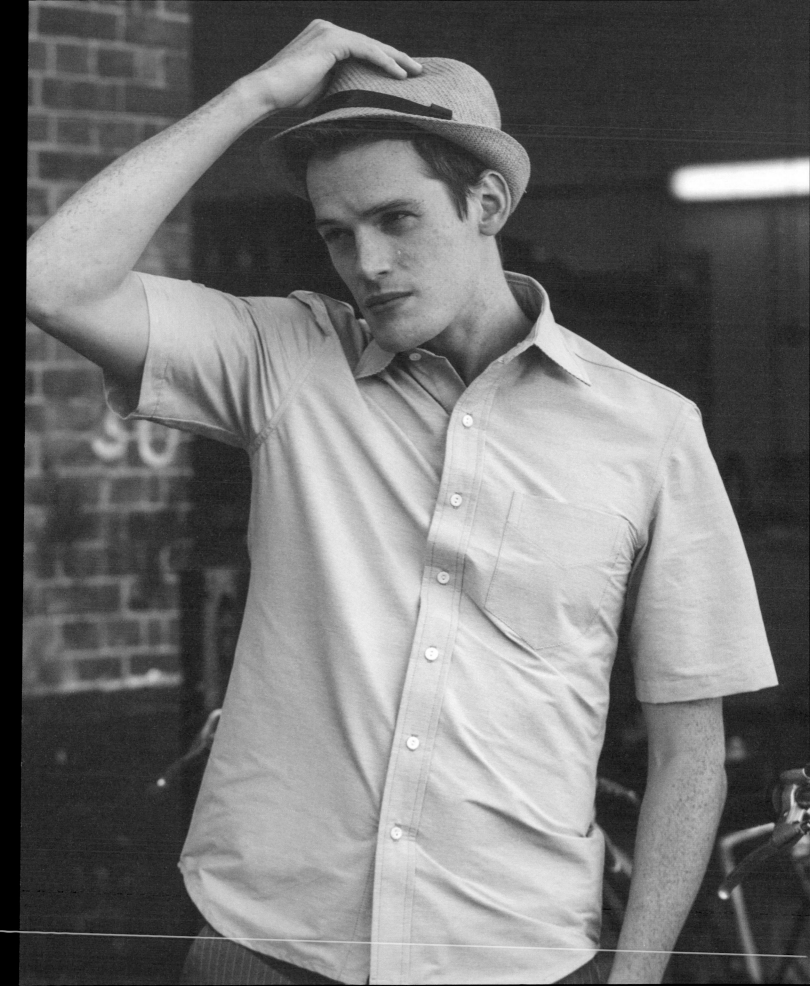

PATTERN PIECES

From pattern sheets A, B, D and F:

1 Back (cut 1 in main fabric)

2 Front (cut 2 in main fabric)

3 Sleeve (cut 2 in main fabric)

4 Collar (cut 2 in main fabric, cut 1 in interfacing)

5 Buttonhole band (cut 1 in main fabric, cut 1 in interfacing)

6 Collar stand (cut 2 in main fabric, cut 1 in interfacing)

7 Cuff (cut 4 in main fabric, cut 2 in interfacing)

8 Yoke (cut 2 in main fabric)

9 Pocket (cut 1 in main fabric)

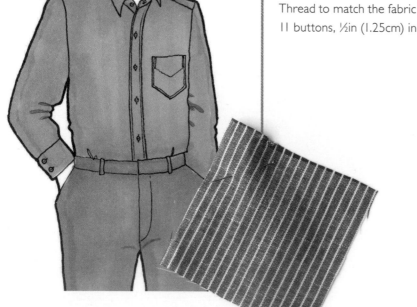

SHIRT

This classic shirt features a yoke and curved hem, double-buttoned cuff sleeves and a single chest pocket. For a more casual, short-sleeved version, see page 38.

FABRIC REQUIRED

Refer to the appropriate column for your clothing size and the fabric width.

FABRIC WIDTH (WITHOUT NAP)	SMALL	MEDIUM	LARGE
36in (90cm)	3yd (2.7m)	3yd (2.7m)	3⅛yd (2.8m)
45in (115cm)	2⅝yd (2.4m)	2¾yd (2.5m)	2¾yd (2.5m)
60in (150cm)	2⅛yd (1.9m)	2¼yd (2m)	2¼yd (2m)
36in (90cm) light- to medium-weight iron-on interfacing	⅞yd (0.8m)	⅞yd (0.8m)	⅞yd (0.8m)

SUGGESTED FABRICS

Cotton shirting, lawn, poplin, linen, chambray, needlecord, denim, light-weight wool, wool mix

SEWING NOTIONS

Thread to match the fabric
11 buttons, ½in (1.25cm) in diameter

SEAM ALLOWANCES

Take ⅝in (1.5cm) seam allowances throughout, unless otherwise stated

FINISHED MEASUREMENTS

Finished back length

S: 28in (71cm)

M: 28⅜in (72cm)

L: 28¾in (73cm)

PATTERN NOTE

The armhole, sleeve and side seams are finished with flat-fell seams. For alternative seam finishes, see page 159.

60in (150cm) wide fabric

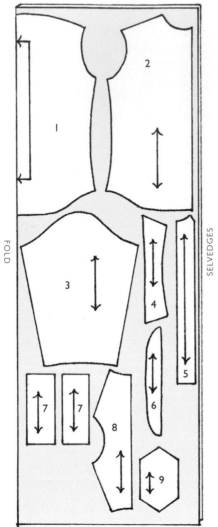

FOLD

SELVEDGES

OPEN FABRIC OUT TO CUT
BUTTONHOLE BAND & POCKET

45in (115cm) wide fabric

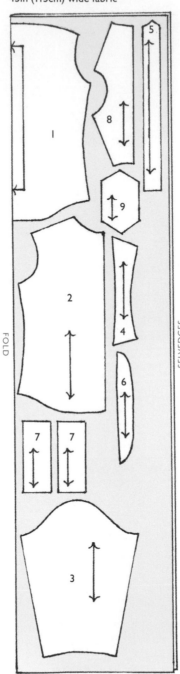

FOLD

SELVEDGES

OPEN FABRIC OUT TO CUT
BUTTONHOLE BAND & POCKET

36in (90cm) wide fabric

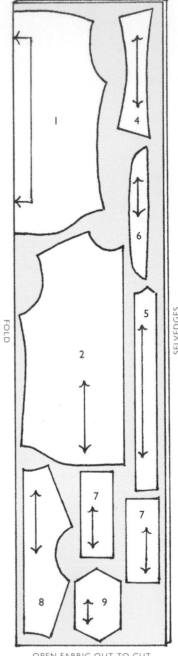

FOLD

SELVEDGES

OPEN FABRIC OUT TO CUT
BUTTONHOLE BAND & POCKET

36in (90cm) wide fabric

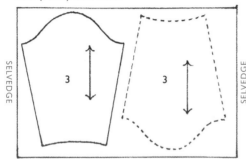

SELVEDGE

SELVEDGE

BROKEN LINES INDICATE REVERSE
SIDE OF PATTERN

1 Staystitch (see page 156) the neck edges of the front and yoke pieces to prevent the fabric from stretching.

Join yoke, front and back

2 With right sides together, pin one yoke piece to the back of the shirt, matching the notches. Place the right side of the remaining yoke piece to the wrong side of the back of the shirt. This will be the yoke facing. Stitch through all the layers, easing the back to fit between the notches. Press the yoke facing up.

3 With the right side of the yoke facing to the wrong side of the front pieces, stitch together at the shoulders, matching the notches. Press the seams towards the yoke facing.

4 Press under ⅝in (1.5cm) on the front edges of the yoke. Press the yoke up. On the outside of the garment, pin the pressed edges of the yoke over the shoulder seams. Topstitch (see page 156) close to the pressed edges.

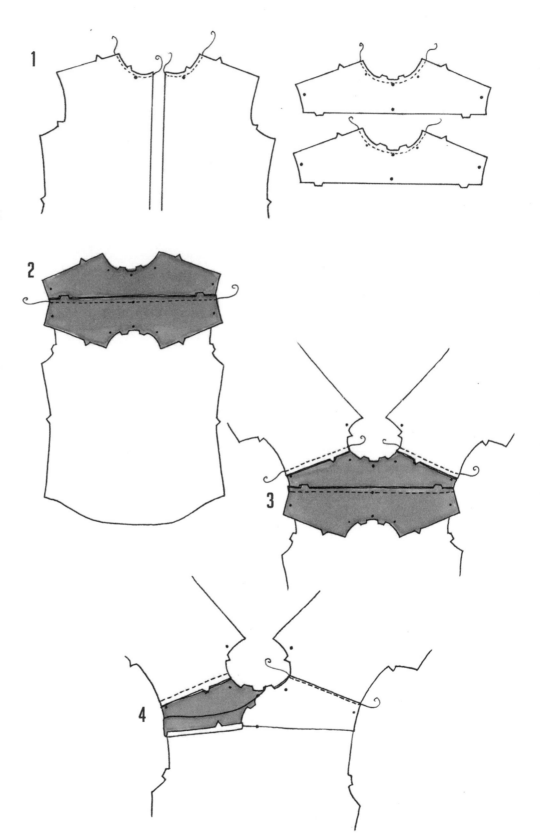

 RIGHT SIDE OF FABRIC

 WRONG SIDE OF FABRIC

 INTERFACING

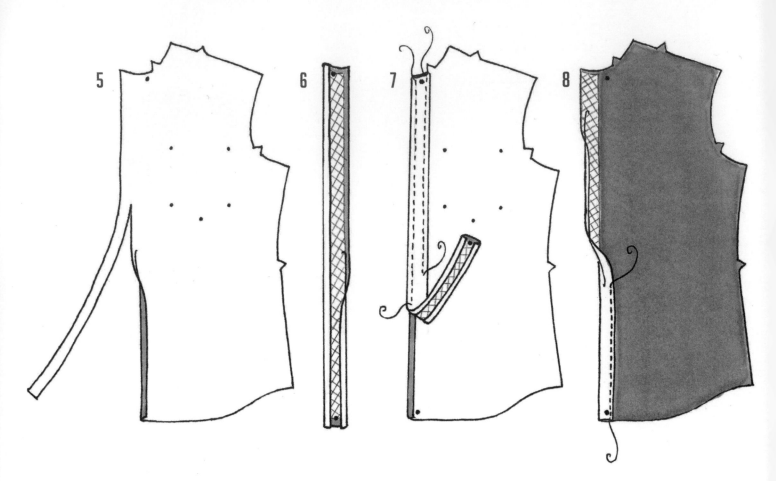

Buttonhole band

5 Trim away 1in (2.5cm) from the left front edge. Turn and press the front edge to the outside along the fold line, indicated on the pattern.

6 Following the manufacturer's instructions, apply iron-on interfacing (see page 145) to the wrong side of the front band. Turn under and press the seam allowances on each long edge of the front band.

7 On the outside of the garment, tack the front band, right side facing up, to the left front of the shirt, matching the centre front dots. Topstitch each side of the front band, ¼in (0.6cm) from the long, pressed edges. Remove the tacking stitches.

Right front facing

8 Following the manufacturer's instructions, apply iron-on interfacing to the wrong side of the right front edge, up to the fold line. Turn under and press ¼in (0.6cm) on the right front edge. Turn the front edge to the inside along the fold line and stitch in place, close to the pressed edge, to form the facing.

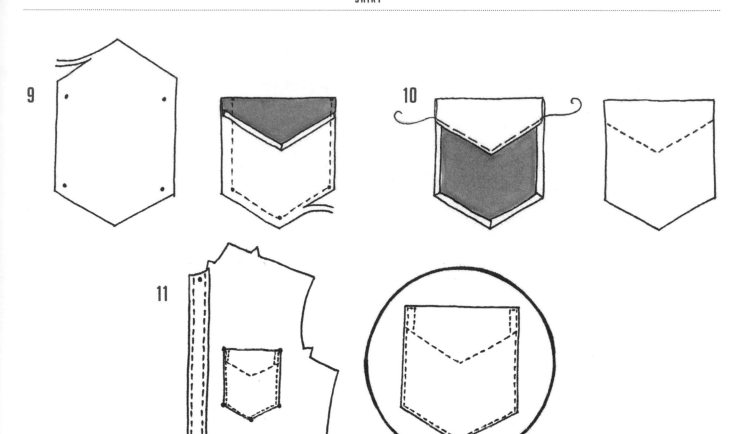

Pocket

9 Trim the seam allowance along the top edges of the pocket to ¼in (0.6cm). Turn under the trimmed seam at the top edges and press. Turn the top of the pocket to the outside along the fold line to form the facing. Stitch along the ⅝in (1.5cm) seam line of the side and lower edges. Trim the seams of the side and lower edges to ¼in (0.6cm).

10 Turn the facing to the inside. Turn under the raw edges along the stitch line from the previous step and press. Tack the facing down, close to the edges. Topstitch along the tacking line, then remove the tacking stitches.

11 Pin the pocket to the right side of the left front, matching the dots. Tack and then sew in place, stitching close to the side and lower edges, forming a narrow rectangle at each side of the top of the pocket.

12

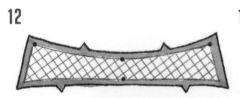

13

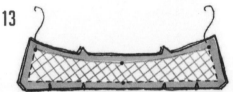

14

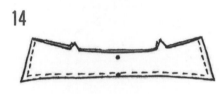

Collar

12 Following the manufacturer's instructions, apply iron-on interfacing to the wrong side of one collar piece. This will be the top collar. The second collar piece will be the under collar.

13 With right sides together, pin the top collar to the under collar. Stitch around the three outer edges. Trim the seams, snip the curves and cut diagonally across the corners (see page 158).

14 Turn the collar right side out and press. Topstitch ¼in (0.6cm) from the stitched edges.

15 Following the manufacturer's instructions, apply iron-on interfacing to the wrong side of one collar stand piece. This will be the collar stand. The second piece will be the collar stand facing. Press under ⅝in (1.5cm) on neck edge of the collar stand. Trim to ¼in (0.6cm).

16 With the right sides together, matching notches and dots, pin and tack the collar to the collar stand facing.

17 With right sides together, pin the collar stand to the collar stand facing, sandwiching the collar in between. Stitch the outer edge between the seam lines. Trim the seam and notch the curves.

18 Turn the collar stand right side out and press. On the inside of the garment, matching notches and dots, pin and stitch the collar stand facing to the neck edge. Trim the seam and snip the curves.

19 On the outside of the garment, pin the pressed edge of the collar stand over the seam, matching the dots. Topstitch close to the pressed edge. Topstitch close to the top edge of the collar stand, starting and ending at the neck edge.

15

16

17

18

19

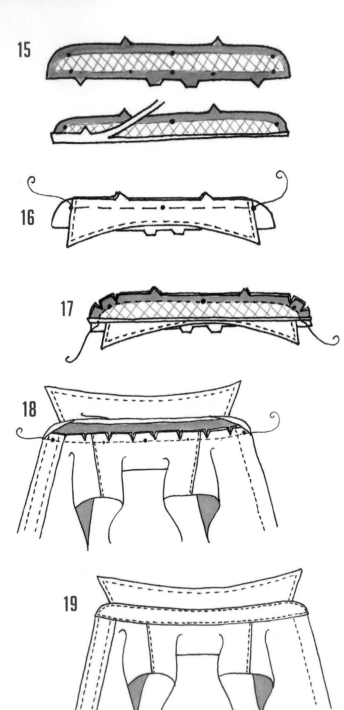

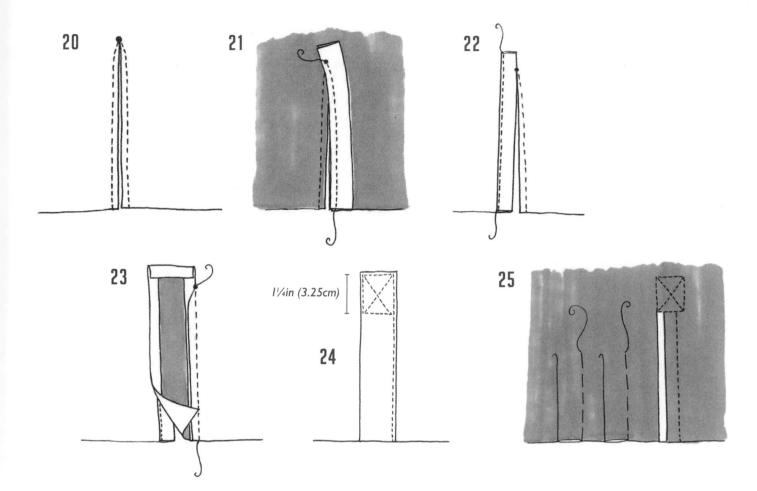

Sleeve openings

20 Staystitch the sleeve, ¼in (0.6cm) each side of the long line indicated on the pattern, starting and ending at the lower edge and tapering to the small dot. Slash between the stitching to the small dot.

Underlap

21 Cut two straight strips of fabric, each measuring 1¼in (3.25cm) wide by 5in (12.75cm) long. With wrong sides together, fold each strip in half lengthways and press. Aligning the raw edges, stitch a folded strip to the staystitching on the wrong side of the back opening of each sleeve, taking a ¼in (0.6cm) seam on the strip.

22 Turn the strip to the outside and stitch in place, close to the folded edge.

Overlap

23 Cut two straight strips of fabric, each measuring 2¼in (5.75cm) wide by 5¾in (14.5cm) long for the overlap. With the right side of the strip to the wrong side of the sleeve, pin and sew the strip to the staystitching on the front side of the sleeve opening, taking a ¼in (0.6cm) seam on the strip. Press the seam towards the strip. Turn under and press ¼in (0.6cm) on the side and top edges of the strip.

24 On the right side of the sleeve, pin the pressed edge of the strip over the seam. Stitch close to the pressed edge. Stitch the top of the strip to the sleeve, forming a rectangle 1¼in (3.25cm) deep, enclosing the top of the underlap. Stitch diagonally across the rectangle to reinforce the top of the opening.

25 Make the pleats in the sleeve by folding along the solid vertical lines, with right sides together, matching the broken lines. Tack along the broken lines. Lay the pleats away from the opening.

Sleeves

26 Run two rows of gathering stitches (see page 162) in between the notches, by hand or using a long machine stitch, working one row along the seam line and the other ¼in (0.6cm) inside the seam line, to ease the fullness of the top of the sleeve.

27 With right sides together, pin the sleeve to the armhole, matching the notches, the seam lines at the underarms, and the centre dot on the sleeve to the dot on the armhole edge of the yoke. Pull up the gathering stitches to fit, adjusting them so they are evenly distributed. Insert plenty of pins to help ease the fullness of the sleeve head. Stitch between the underarm seams. Press the seam towards the armhole. Trim the edge on the armhole and finish the flat-fell seam on the inside of the shirt, easing the fabric on the sleeve head. The finished seam will look neater on the outside of the garment. Remove the gathering stitches.

Sleeve and side seams

28 With right sides together, stitch the sleeve and side seams, matching notches and underarm seams. Press the seam towards the back. Trim the edge at the back of the shirt and sleeve. Finish the flat-fell seam on the inside of the garment, starting at the hem and working slowly into the sleeve. Make sure the needle is in the work each time you pause the machine.

Cuffs

29 Following the manufacturer's instructions, apply iron-on interfacing (see page 145) to the wrong side of one cuff piece. Press under ⅝in (1.5cm) along the upper edge of the faced cuff piece. Trim to ¼in (0.6cm). The remaining piece will be the cuff facing.

30 With right sides together, pin and stitch the cuff facing to the cuff around the outer edges. Trim the seams and cut diagonally across the corners, taking care not to cut into the stitching.

31 Turn right side out and press. With right side of the cuff facing to the wrong side of the sleeve, pin and stitch together, matching the notches and the small dot to the sleeve seam. Trim and press the seam towards the cuff facing.

32 On the outside of the sleeve, pin the pressed edge of the cuff over the seam. Stitch close to the pressed edge. Topstitch ¼in (0.6cm) from the top and outer edges of the cuff. Remove the tacking stitches.

Hem

33 Staystitch along the ⅝in (1.5cm) seam line at the lower edge. Turn the lower edge to the inside along the staystitching. Turn under the raw edge and press. Stitch in place.

Finishing off

34 Finish by working buttonholes by hand or machine (see page 168) on the left front. Make a horizontal buttonhole on the collar and six vertical buttonholes down the front of the shirt, as indicated on the pattern. Attach the buttons to the right front to correspond with the buttonholes. Work two buttonholes in each cuff by hand or machine, as indicated on the pattern. Mark the position of buttons on the cuffs to correspond with the buttonholes. Attach the buttons to the cuffs.

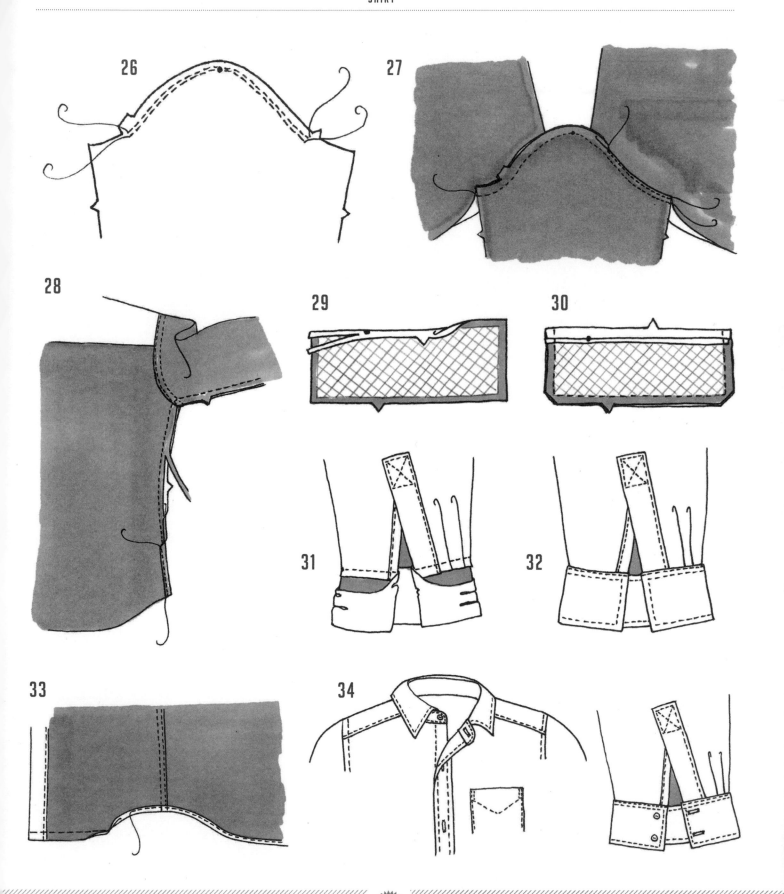

SUMMER SHIRT

This short-sleeved shirt can be made with a bold print for casual wear and beach parties, or in a light-weight cotton shirting for warm days in the office.

PATTERN PIECES

Use pieces for Shirt, from pattern sheets A, B, D and F:

1 Back (cut 1 in main fabric)
2 Front (cut 2 in main fabric, cut 1 in interfacing for right front facing only)
3 Sleeve (cut 2 in main fabric)
4 Collar (cut 2 in main fabric, cut 1 in interfacing)
5 Buttonhole band (cut 1 in main fabric, cut 1 in interfacing)
6 Collar stand (cut 2 in main fabric, cut 1 in interfacing)
8 Yoke (cut 2 in main fabric)
9 Pocket (cut 1 in main fabric)

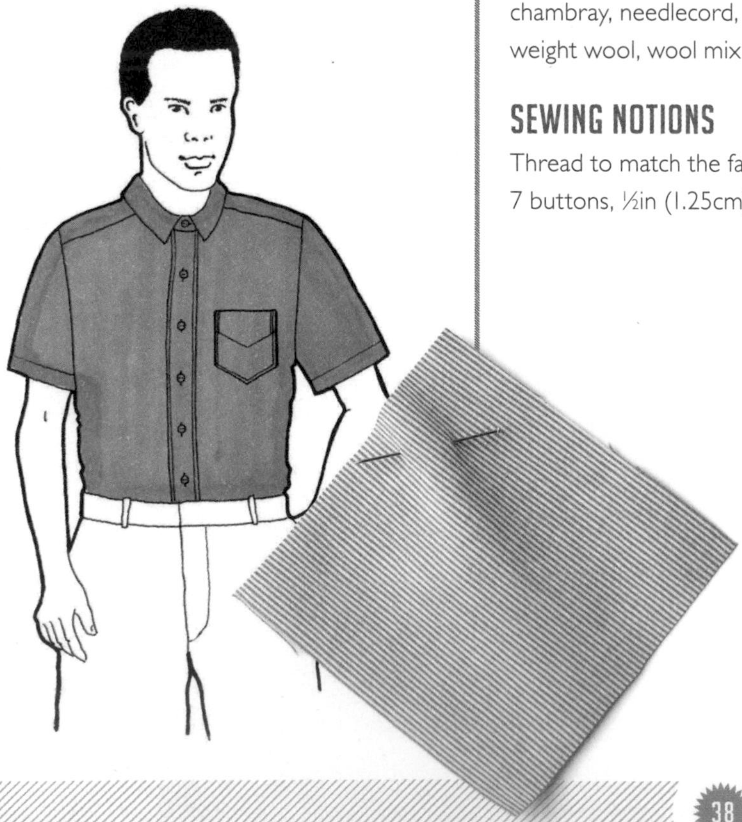

FABRIC REQUIRED

Refer to the appropriate column for your clothing size and the fabric width.

FABRIC WIDTH (WITHOUT NAP)	SMALL	MEDIUM	LARGE
36in (90cm)	2⅝yd (2.4m)	2¾yd (2.5m)	2¾yd (2.5m)
45in (115cm)	2⅛yd (1.9m)	2⅛yd (1.9m)	2¼yd (2m)
60in (150cm)	1¾yd (1.6m)	1⅞yd (1.7m)	1⅞yd (1.7m)
36in (90cm) light- to medium-weight iron-on interfacing	⅞yd (0.8m)	⅞yd (0.8m)	⅞yd (0.8m)

SUGGESTED FABRICS

Cotton shirting, lawn, poplin, linen, chambray, needlecord, denim, light-weight wool, wool mix

SEWING NOTIONS

Thread to match the fabric
7 buttons, ½in (1.25cm) in diameter

SEAM ALLOWANCES

Take ⅝in (1.5cm) seam allowances throughout, unless otherwise stated

FINISHED MEASUREMENTS

Finished back length
S: 28in (71cm)
M: 28⅜in (72cm)
L: 28¾in (73cm)

PATTERN NOTE

The armhole, sleeve and side seams are finished with flat-fell seams. For alternative seam finishes, see page 159.

60in (150cm) wide fabric

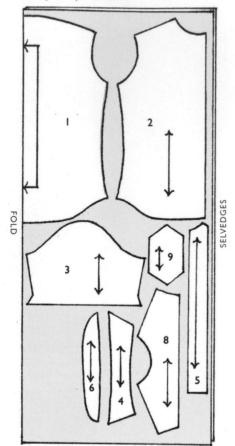

FOLD

SELVEDGES

OPEN FABRIC OUT TO CUT
BUTTONHOLE BAND & POCKET

45in (115cm) wide fabric

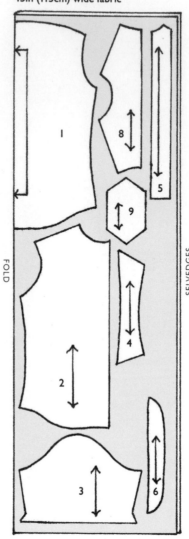

FOLD

SELVEDGES

OPEN FABRIC OUT TO CUT
BUTTONHOLE BAND & POCKET

36in (90cm) wide fabric

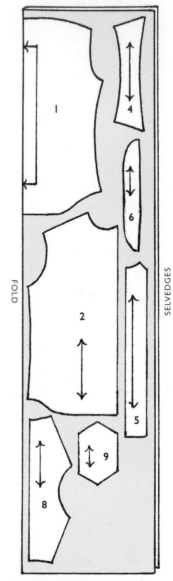

FOLD

SELVEDGES

OPEN FABRIC OUT TO CUT
BUTTONHOLE BAND & POCKET

36in (90cm) wide fabric

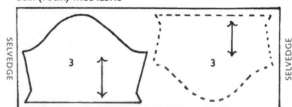

SELVEDGE

SELVEDGE

BROKEN LINES INDICATE REVERSE SIDE OF PATTERN

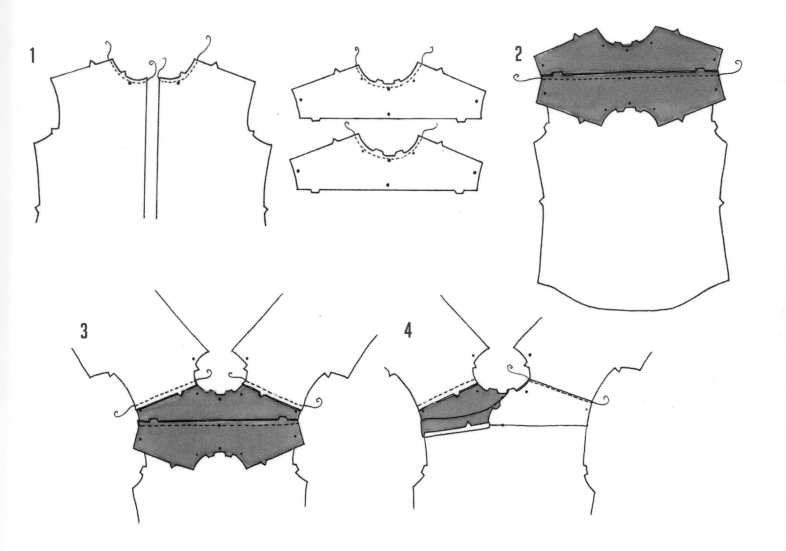

RIGHT SIDE OF FABRIC

WRONG SIDE OF FABRIC

INTERFACING

1 Staystitch (see page 156) the neck edges of the front and yoke pieces to prevent the fabric from stretching.

Join yoke, front and back

2 With right sides together, pin one yoke piece to the back of the shirt, matching the notches. Place the right side of the remaining yoke piece to the wrong side of the back of the shirt. This will be the yoke facing. Stitch through all the layers, easing the back to fit between the notches. Press the yoke facing up.

3 With the right side of the yoke facing to the wrong side of the front pieces, stitch together at the shoulders, matching the notches. Press the seams towards the yoke facing.

4 Press under ⅝in. (1.5cm) on the front edges of the yoke. Press the yoke up. On the outside of the garment, pin the pressed edges of the yoke over the shoulder seams. Topstitch (see page 156) close to the pressed edges.

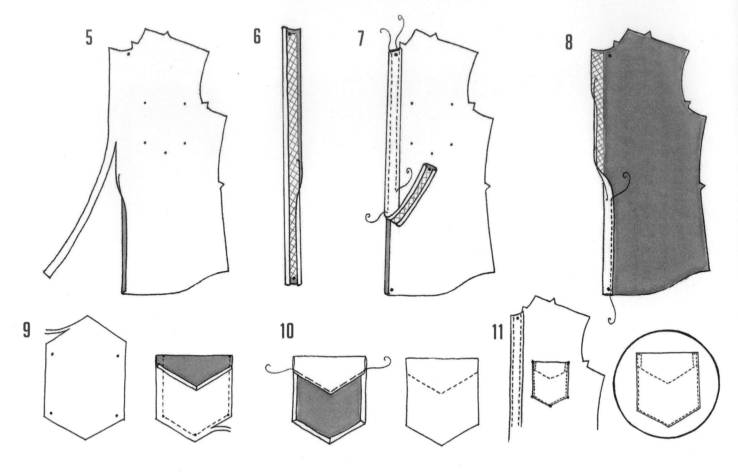

Buttonhole band

5 Trim away 1in (2.5cm) from the left front edge. Turn and press the front edge to the outside along the fold line, indicated on the pattern.

6 Following the manufacturer's instructions, apply iron-on interfacing (see page 145) to the wrong side of the front band. Turn under and press the seam allowances on each long edge of the front band.

7 On the outside of the garment, tack the front band, right side facing up, to the left front of the shirt, matching the centre front dots. Topstitch each side of the front band, ¼in (0.6cm) from the long, pressed edges. Remove tacking stitches.

Right front facing

8 Following the manufacturer's instructions, apply iron-on interfacing to the wrong side of the right front edge, up to the fold line. Turn under and press ¼in (0.6cm) on the right front edge. Turn the front edge to the inside along the fold line and stitch in place, close to the pressed edge, to form the facing.

Pocket

9 Trim the seam allowance along the top edges of the pocket to ¼in (0.6cm). Turn under the trimmed seam at the top edges and press. Turn the top of the pocket to the outside along the fold line to form the facing. Stitch

along the ⅝in (1.5cm) seam line of the side and lower edges. Trim the seams of the side and lower edges to ¼in (0.6cm).

10 Turn the facing to the inside. Turn under the raw edges along the stitch line from the previous step and press. Tack the facing down, close to the edges. Topstitch along the tacking line, then remove the tacking stitches.

11 Pin the pocket to the right side of the left front, matching the dots. Tack and sew in place, stitching close to the side and lower edges, forming a narrow rectangle at each side of the top of the pocket.

Collar

12 Following the manufacturer's instructions, apply iron-on interfacing to the wrong side of one collar piece. This will be the top collar. The second collar piece will be the under collar.

13 With right sides together, pin the top collar to the under collar. Stitch around the three outer edges. Trim the seams, snip the curves and cut diagonally across the corners (see page 158).

14 Turn the collar right side out and press. Topstitch ¼in (0.6cm) from the stitched edges.

15 Following the manufacturer's instructions, apply iron-on interfacing to the wrong side of one collar stand piece. This will be the collar stand. The second piece will be the collar stand facing. Press under ⅝in (1.5cm) on neck edge of the collar stand. Trim to ¼in (0.6cm).

16 With the right sides together, matching notches and dots, pin and tack the collar to the collar stand facing.

17 With right sides together, pin the collar stand to the collar stand facing, sandwiching the collar in between. Stitch the outer edge between the seam lines. Trim the seam and notch the curves.

18 Turn the collar stand right side out and press. On the inside of the garment, matching notches and dots, pin and stitch the collar stand facing to the neck edge. Trim the seam and snip the curves.

19 On the outside of the garment, pin the pressed edge of the collar stand over the seam, matching the dots. Topstitch close to the pressed edge. Topstitch close to the top edge of the collar stand, starting and ending at the neck edge.

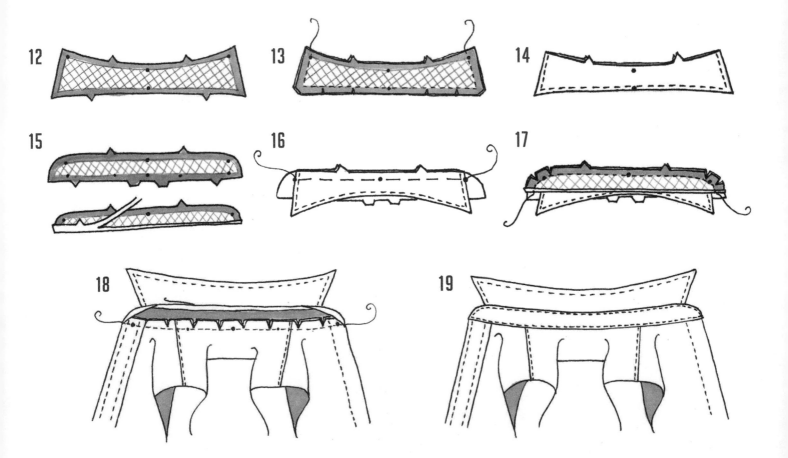

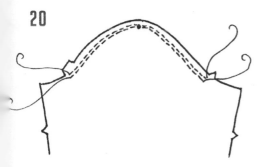

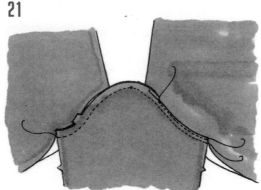

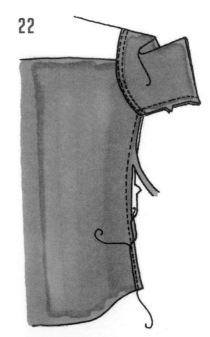

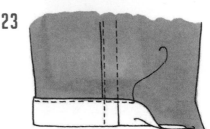

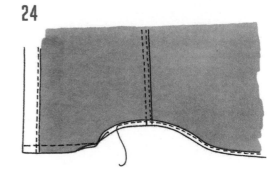

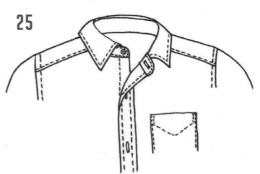

Sleeves

20 Run two rows of gathering stitches (see page 162) in between the notches, by hand or using a long machine stitch, working one row along the seam line and the other ¼in (0.6cm) inside the seam line, to ease the fullness of the top of the sleeve.

21 With right sides together, pin the sleeve to the armhole, matching the notches, the seam lines at the underarms, and the centre dot on the sleeve to the dot on the armhole edge of the yoke. Pull up the gathering stitches to fit, adjusting them so they are evenly distributed. Insert plenty of pins to help ease the fullness of the sleeve head. Stitch between the underarm seams. Press the seam towards the armhole. Trim the edge on the armhole and finish the flat-fell seam on the inside of the shirt, easing the fabric on the sleeve head. The finished seam will look neater on the outside of the garment. Remove the gathering stitches.

Sleeve and side seams

22 With right sides together, stitch the sleeve and side seams, matching notches and underarm seams. Press

the seam towards the back. Trim the edge at the back of the shirt and sleeve. Finish the flat-fell seam on the inside of the garment, starting at the hem and working slowly into the sleeve. Make sure the needle is in the work each time you pause the machine.

Sleeve hem

23 Turn up the sleeve hems and press. Turn under and press ¼in (0.6cm) on the lower edge of the sleeve. Stitch close to the turned raw edges.

Hem

24 Staystitch along the ⅝in (1.5cm) seam line at the lower edge. Turn the lower edge to the inside along the staystitching. Turn under the raw edge and press. Stitch in place.

Finishing off

25 Finish by working buttonholes by hand or machine (see page 168) on the left front. Make a horizontal buttonhole on the collar and six vertical buttonholes down the front of the shirt, as indicated on the pattern. Attach the buttons to the right front to correspond with the buttonholes.

WAISTCOAT

With its V-shaped neckline and two welt pockets this waistcoat will lend any outfit a distinctive look. The back matches the lining and features an adjustable belt.

PATTERN PIECES

From pattern sheet C:

10 Front (cut 2 in main fabric)

11 Front facing (cut 2 in main fabric, cut 2 in interfacing)

12 Welt (cut 2 in main fabric, cut 2 in interfacing)

13 Back (cut 4 in lining fabric)

14 Pocket (cut 2 in lining fabric)

15 Belt (cut 2 in lining fabric)

16 Front lining (cut 2 in lining fabric)

FABRIC REQUIRED

Refer to the appropriate column for your clothing size and the fabric width.

FABRIC WIDTH (WITHOUT NAP)	SMALL	MEDIUM	LARGE
36in (90cm)			
Main fabric:	⅞yd (0.8m)	⅞yd (0.8m)	⅞yd (0.8m)
Lining fabric:	2¼yd (2m)	2¼yd (2m)	2¼yd (2m)
45in (115cm)			
Main fabric:	⅞yd (0.8m)	⅞yd (0.8m)	⅞yd (0.8m)
Lining fabric:	2¼yd (2m)	2¼yd (2m)	2¼yd (2m)
60in (150cm)			
Main fabric:	¾yd (0.7m)	¾yd (0.7m)	¾yd (0.7m)
Lining fabric:	1⅜yd (1.3m)	1⅜yd (1.3m)	1⅜yd (1.3m)
36in (90cm) light- to medium-weight iron-on interfacing	¾yd (0.7m)	¾yd (0.7m)	¾yd (0.7m)

SUGGESTED FABRICS

For main fabric: Tweed, corduroy, denim, gabardine, linen

For lining: Satin, cotton shirting

SEWING NOTIONS

Thread to match the fabric

5 buttons, ½in (1.25cm) in diameter

Buckle with an interior width of 1in (2.5cm)

SEAM ALLOWANCES

Take ⅝in (1.5cm) seam allowances throughout, unless otherwise stated

FINISHED MEASUREMENTS

Finished back length

S: 20⅝in (52.5cm)

M: 21⅛in (53.75cm)

L: 21⅝in (55cm)

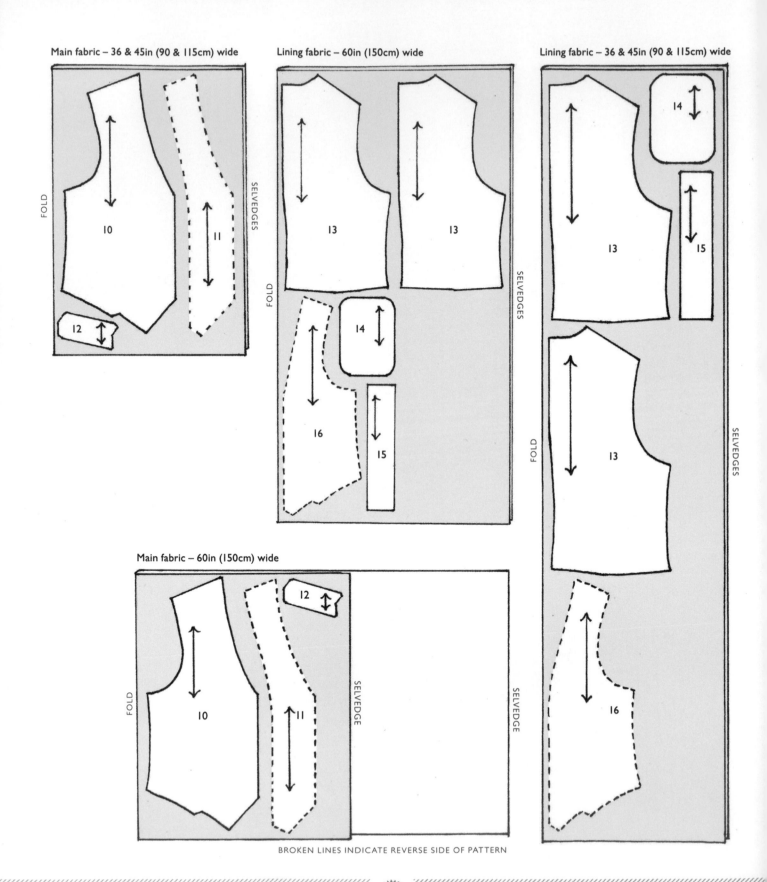

Main fabric – 36 & 45in (90 & 115cm) wide

Lining fabric – 60in (150cm) wide

Lining fabric – 36 & 45in (90 & 115cm) wide

Main fabric – 60in (150cm) wide

BROKEN LINES INDICATE REVERSE SIDE OF PATTERN

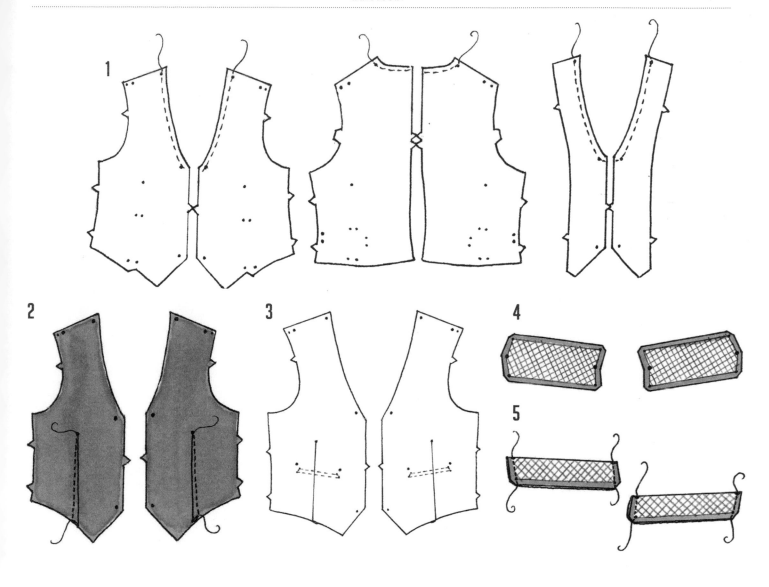

RIGHT SIDE
OF FABRIC

WRONG SIDE
OF FABRIC

INTERFACING

1 Staystitch (see page 156) the neck edges of the front and back pieces and the front facings to prevent the fabric from stretching.

Front

2 Stitch the darts on the front pieces (see page 161). Press the darts towards the centre front.

Pockets

3 Stitch along the pocket lines, in between the small dots, to reinforce the openings.

4 Following the manufacturer's instructions, apply iron-on interfacing to the wrong side of each welt.

5 With right sides together, fold each welt along the line indicated on the pattern and stitch the short ends along the ¼in (0.6cm) seam line.

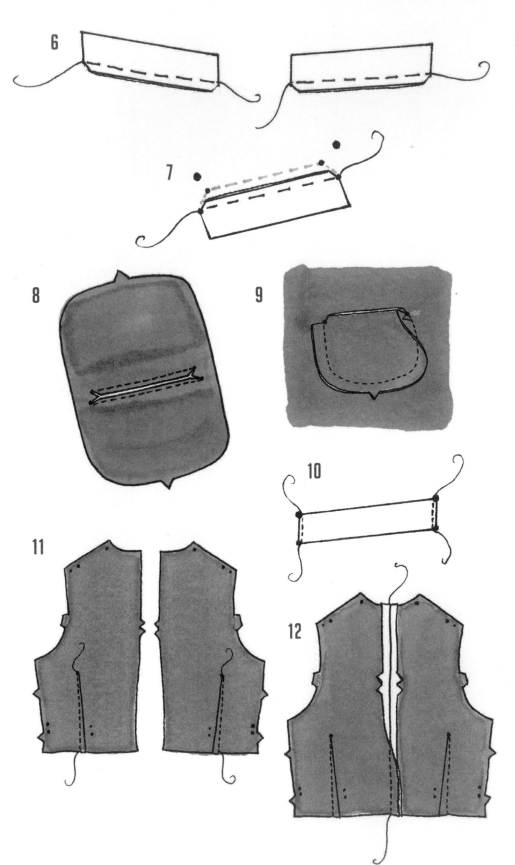

6 Turn the welts right side out and press. Tack the raw edges together on each welt.

7 On the outside of the front pieces, tack the welt to the lower stitching line of the pocket, matching the small dots.

8 With right sides together, pin the pocket to the front, on top of the welt, matching the small dots. The ends of the top line taper slightly, so they will not show when the welt is pressed up. Stitch along the stitching lines indicated on the pattern. Do not stitch across the ends. Slash the pocket and front on the line indicated on the pattern to within ⅜in (1cm) of both ends. Snip diagonally into the corners, taking care not to go through the stitches.

9 Draw the pocket lining through the slash to the wrong side of the front pieces and press. With right sides together, fold the pocket, matching the notches and raw edges. Stitch the outer edges of the pocket together, catching the triangles at each end of the openings in the stitching.

10 On the outside of the garment, press the welt up, matching the medium dots. Sew the sides of the welt to the front, stitching close to the edges.

Back

11 Stitch the darts on the back pieces (see page 161). Press the darts towards the centre back.

12 With right sides together, matching the notches, pin and stitch the centre back seam. Press the seam open.

13

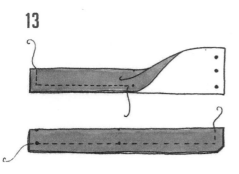

14

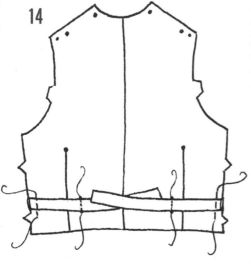

15

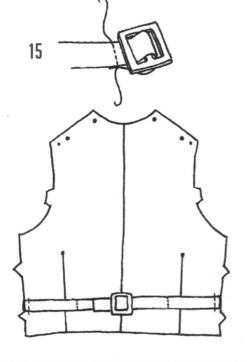

Belt

13 With right sides together, fold the belt along the line indicated on the pattern. Stitch the edges, leaving the short end with the medium dots open to turn. Trim the seams and snip diagonally across the corners, taking care not to cut into the stitching.

14 Turn the belt pieces right side out and press. Tack the belt pieces to the right side of the back of the waistcoat, aligning the raw edges, matching the dots and with the folded edge of the belt at the top. Stitch the belt to the back between the small dots.

15 Sew the buckle to the left belt so it is in line with the centre back seam. Thread the right belt through the buckle.

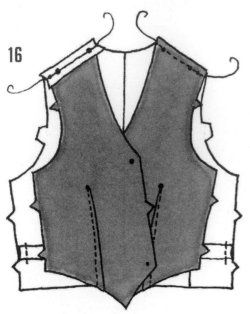

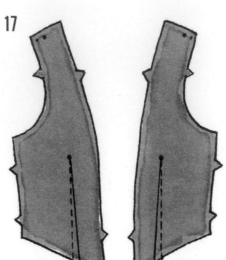

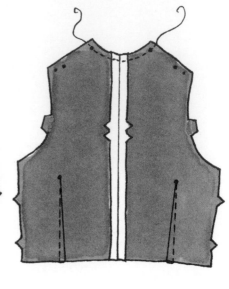

Join front to back

16 With right sides together, matching the small and medium dots, pin and stitch the front pieces to the back at the shoulder seams, easing the back shoulders to fit between the medium dots. Press seams open.

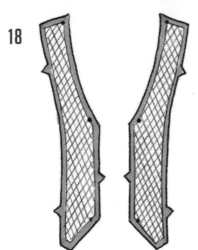

Attach lining

17 Staystitch (see page 156) the neck edges of the back lining pieces to prevent the fabric from stretching. Stitch the darts of the front and back lining pieces. Press the front darts towards the centre front and the back darts towards the centre back. With right sides together, stitch the centre back seam of the lining.

18 Following the manufacturer's instructions, apply iron-on interfacing (see page 145) to the wrong side of the left and right front facings.

19 With right sides together, matching notches, pin and stitch the front lining pieces to the facings. Press seams towards the lining.

20 With right sides together, matching notches, pin and stitch the front lining pieces to the back lining at the shoulder seams, easing the back shoulders to fit between the medium dots. Press seams open.

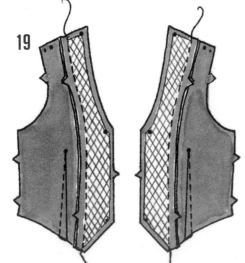

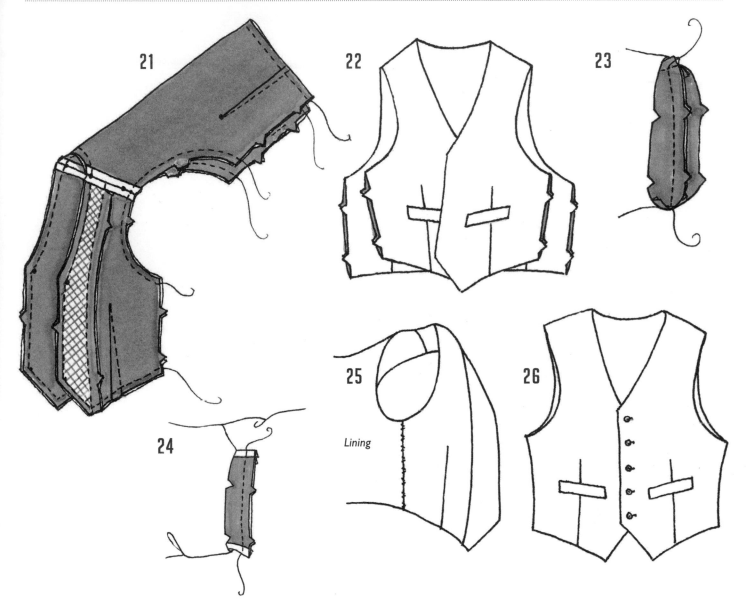

21 With right sides together, matching notches and seams, pin and stitch the lining to the garment around the fronts, neck, armholes and lower edges, leaving the sides open. Trim the seams and corners, and snip the curves (see page 158).

22 Turn right side out through a side opening in the back of the waistcoat and push the fronts out through the shoulders. Press well.

Side seams

23 With right sides together, matching notches, stitch the back and front pieces at the side seams, leaving the lining open.

24 Reach in through one open side seam and pull the other side seam through. Stitch the side seam of the lining and push back in place.

25 Turn under the seam allowance on the remaining side seam of the lining and slipstitch (see page 154) to close.

Finishing off

26 Work buttonholes by hand or machine (see page 168) on the left front, as indicated on the pattern. Lap the left front of the waistcoat over the right, matching the centre fronts. Mark the position of buttons to correspond with the buttonholes. Attach the buttons to the right front (see page 169).

TROUSERS

The pocket and zip are inserted first, to make it easier to sew the main seams together. A wider seam allowance at the back allows for alteration of the waistline.

PATTERN PIECES

From pattern sheets A, B, D and E:

17 Front (cut 2 in main fabric)
18 Back pocket welt (cut 2 in main fabric, cut 4 in interfacing)
19 Back pocket facing (cut 2 in main fabric)
20 Back (cut 2 in main fabric)
21 Fly (cut 2 in main fabric, cut 2 in interfacing; cut 1 in lining fabric for right fly facing)
22 Front pocket facing (cut 2 in main fabric)
23 Waistband (cut 2 in main fabric, cut 2 in interfacing)
24 Side piece (cut 2 in main fabric)
25 Back pocket (cut 2 in lining fabric)
26 Front pocket (cut 2 in lining fabric)

FABRIC REQUIRED

Refer to the appropriate column for your clothing size and the fabric width.

FABRIC WIDTH (WITHOUT NAP)	SMALL	MEDIUM	LARGE
36in (90cm)			
Main fabric: Lining fabric:	**2⅝yd (2.4m)** **1yd (0.9m)**	**2¾yd (2.5m)** **1yd (0.9m)**	**2¾yd (2.5m)** **1yd (0.9m)**
45in (115cm)			
Main fabric: Lining fabric:	**2⅜yd (2.2m)** **1yd (0.9m)**	**2½yd (2.3m)** **1yd (0.9m)**	**2½yd (2.3m)** **1yd (0.9m)**
60in (150cm)			
Main fabric: Lining fabric:	**2⅛yd (1.9m)** **1yd (0.9m)**	**2⅛yd (1.9m)** **1yd (0.9m)**	**2¼yd (2m)** **1yd (0.9m)**
36in (90cm) light- to medium-weight iron-on interfacing	***½yd (0.5m)***	***½yd (0.5m)***	***½yd (0.5m)***

SUGGESTED FABRICS

For main fabric: Linen, denim, twill, corduroy, tweed, light- to medium-weight wool, suiting
For lining: Cotton poplin, cotton mix

SEWING NOTIONS

Thread to match the fabric
8in (20cm) closed-end zip
⅜in (1cm) hook and bar fastening
12yd (11m) of ⅝in (1.5cm) wide bias binding for neatening the seams

PATTERN NOTE

The side, inside leg and crotch seams are neatened as they are stitched with bound edges or the Hong Kong seam finish (see page 159).

SEAM ALLOWANCES

Take ⅝in (1.5cm) seam allowances throughout, apart from the centre back seam that increases to 1¼in (3cm) at the waist

FINISHED MEASUREMENTS

Finished side length from top of waistband
S: 42in (107cm)
M: 42¾in (108.5cm)
L: 43⅓in (110cm)

Width of hem
S: 15⅝in (39.6cm)
M: 16in (40.8cm)
L: 16⅝in (42.2cm)

Main fabric – 36in (90cm) wide

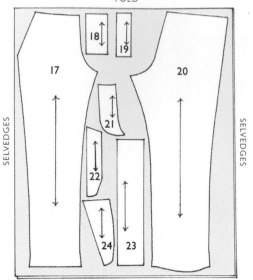

Lining fabric – 36–60in (90–150cm) wide

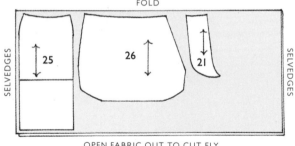

OPEN FABRIC OUT TO CUT FLY

Main fabric – 45in (115cm) wide

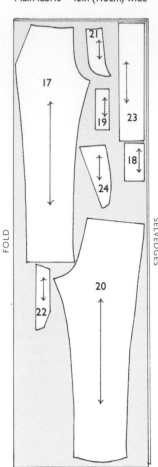

Main fabric – 60in (150cm) wide

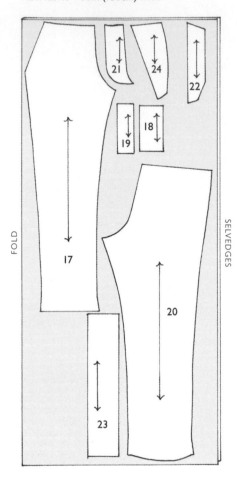

Interfacing – 36in (90cm) wide

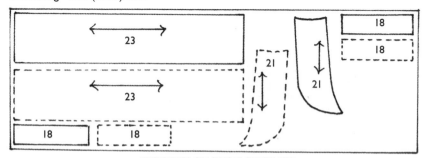

CUT PIECES ON SINGLE THICKNESS
BROKEN LINES INDICATE REVERSE SIDE OF PATTERN

Front and fly

1 With right sides together, stitch along the seam of the front crotch for around 1in (2.5cm) from the medium dot. Stitch over the first line of stitching once more to reinforce the seam.

2 Snip ⅜in (1cm) at the medium dot on the right front only. Turn under and press ⅜in (1cm) along the right front above the snip.

3 Pin the wrong side of the right front over the closed zip, so the lower end of the zip is ¼in (0.6cm) above the medium dot and the pressed edge of the front is close to the teeth of the zip. Tack in place.

4 Following the manufacturer's instructions, apply iron-on interfacing to the wrong side of the left fly. Neaten the outside edge of the fly with binding (see page 166).

5 With right sides together, pin the left fly to the left front opening, matching the dots and notches. Stitch to the medium dot at the base of the opening. Snip the left trouser front to the medium dot. Trim the seam above the snip.

6 Press the seam towards the fly facing. Sew the seam to the facing, stitching to the medium dot, close to the previous line of stitches.

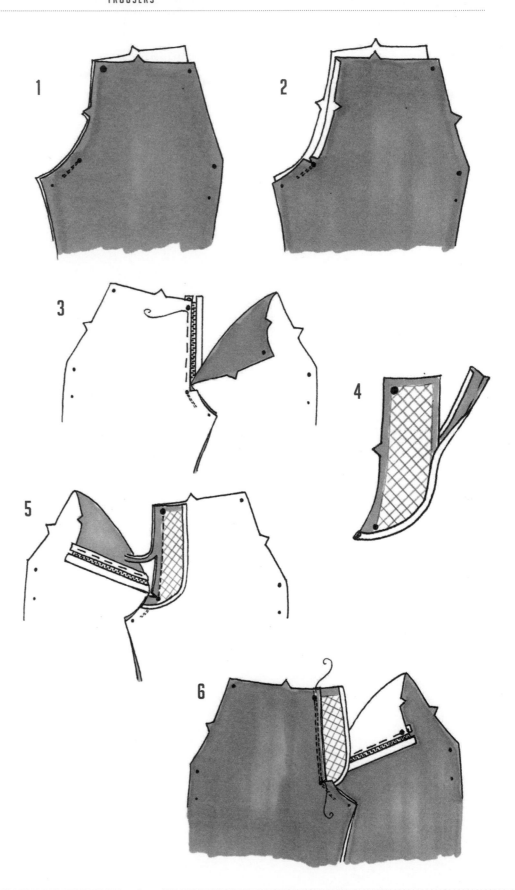

RIGHT SIDE
OF FABRIC

WRONG SIDE
OF FABRIC

INTERFACING

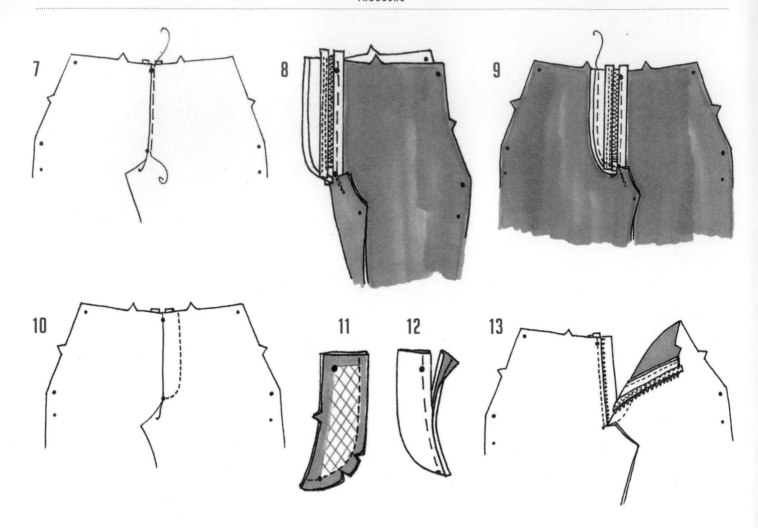

7 Press the fly to the inside. Lap the left front over the right, matching the dots. The left front will overlap the right by around ¼in (0.6cm). Tack the fronts together.

8 With the right sides of the garment together, open out the left fly. Tack the zip to the left fly. Stitch the zip to the left fly, close to the teeth, using a zipper foot. Stitch a second row ¼in (0.6cm) from the first row of stitching.

9 Press the fly to the inside of the garment. Tack the fly to the inside, along the ⅝in (1.5cm) seam line of the curved edge.

10 On the right side of the garment, topstitch the left front along the tacking line. Remove the tacking stitches.

11 Following the manufacturer's instructions, apply iron-on interfacing to the wrong side of the right fly. With right sides together and matching the dots, pin and stitch the right fly and right fly facing pieces together along the curved edge, leaving the top and front edges open. Trim the seam and notch the curve.

12 Turn the fly right side out and press. Tack the raw edges together. Neaten the raw edges with binding. Remove the tacking stitches.

13 Tack the right front edge over the bound edge of the right fly, matching the dots and aligning the raw, upper edges. On the outside of the garment, stitch close to the right front edge, sewing through all layers using a zipper foot. Remove the tacking stitches.

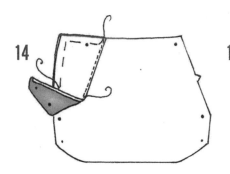 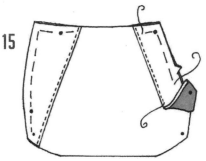  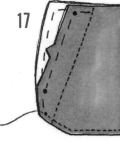

Front pockets

14 Press under ¼in (0.6cm) on the long, straight edge of the pocket side piece. Pin the wrong side of the side piece to the right side of the pocket, aligning the raw edges and the pressed edge of the side piece with the line indicated on the pattern. Stitch close to the pressed edge of the side piece. Tack the raw edges together.

15 Press under ¼in (0.6cm) on the long, straight edge of the pocket facing. Pin the wrong side of the facing to the right side of the pocket, aligning the raw edges and the pressed edge of the facing with the line indicated on the pattern. Stitch close to the pressed edge of the facing. Tack the raw edges together.

16 With wrong sides together, fold the pocket along the line indicated on the pattern, matching the small dots. Join the lower edges with a French seam (see page 160), stitching from the small dot to the folded edge, working ¼in (0.6cm) from the raw edge. Snip to the small dot. Trim the seam and notch the curve below the small dot.

17 Turn wrong side out and press. Stitch ⅜in (1cm) seam from the small dot to enclose the edges, finishing the French seam.

18 With right sides together, pin and stitch the faced edges of the pockets to the front of the trousers, matching the notches and dots. Trim the seam.

19 Press the pocket to the inside. On the outside of the garment, topstitch ¼in (0.6cm) from the edge of the pocket, pivoting the needle when it is parallel to the medium dot and stitching to the medium dot.

20 Tack the top and side edges of the pocket to the trousers to hold them in place while finishing the garment.

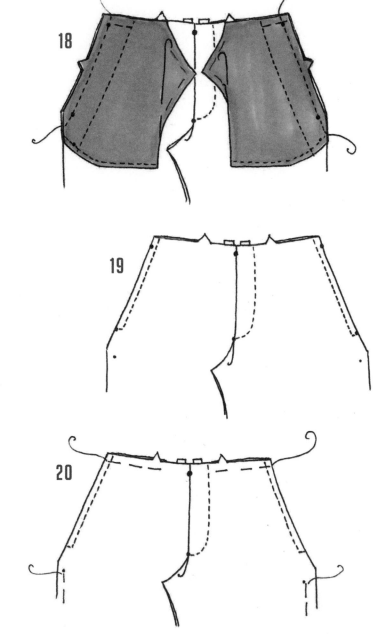

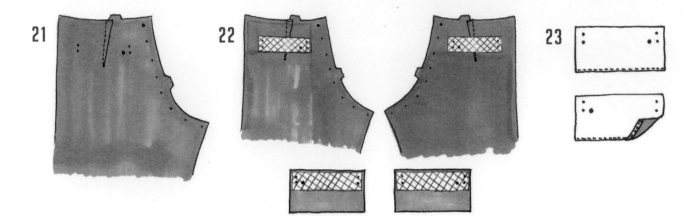

Back

21 Stitch the darts (see page 161) in the trouser back pieces and press towards the centre back.

Back pockets

22 Following the manufacturer's instructions, apply iron-on interfacing to the wrong side of the trouser backs and the welts, matching the dots.

23 Turn under and press ¼in (0.6cm) on the lower edge of the welts. Stitch close to the pressed edges.

24 Press under ¼in (0.6cm) on the long edge of the pocket facing without dots. Pin the wrong side of the facing to the top half of the right side of the pocket, matching the small dots. Stitch close to the pressed edge of the facing. Tack the raw edges to the pocket. Press ¼in (0.6cm) to the right side of the pocket along the long edges. Stitch close to the pressed edges.

25 With wrong sides together, matching the dots, pin the pocket to the trouser back. Stitch along the pocket lines, between the small dots.

26 With right sides together, pin the welt of the pocket to the back, matching the dots. Stitch along the stitching lines, between the small dots. Do not stitch across the ends. Slash the welt, trouser back and pocket on the line indicated on the pattern to within ⅜in (1cm) of both ends. Snip diagonally into the corners, taking care not to cut through the stitches.

27 Draw the welt through the slash to the wrong side of the back pieces. Press the raw edges away from the pocket opening.

28 Press the welt up. Press a fold in the welt piece so the crease is in line with the top of the rectangular opening, forming the welt of the pocket

29 Stitch the triangular ends on each side of the opening to the ends of the welt.

30 On the outside of the garment, stitch along the lower edge of the welt, sinking the stitches in the seam line.

31 On the inside of the garment, fold the pocket away from the garment and stitch the pressed edge of the welt to the pocket.

32 With right sides together, fold the pocket along the line indicated on the pattern, matching the small dots. Stitch the sides of the pocket together, ⅜in (1cm) from the edges below the small dots, catching the ends of the welts in the stitches. Work a second row of stitches close to the pressed edges.

33 On the outside of the garment, fold the waist edge down and pin the pocket together, matching the small dots. Tack the layers together along the seam line. Stitch along the seam line, through all layers.

34 On the outside of the garment, stitch along the top and at each end of the welt, sinking the stitches in the seam line and sewing through all the layers.

35 Tack the top edges of the pocket and trousers together.

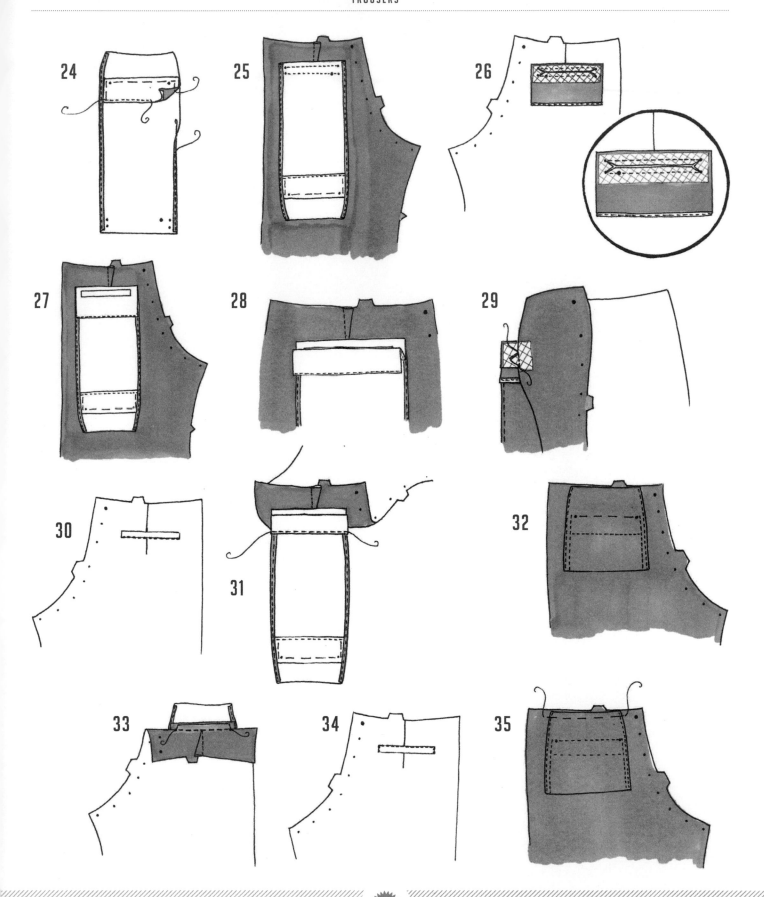

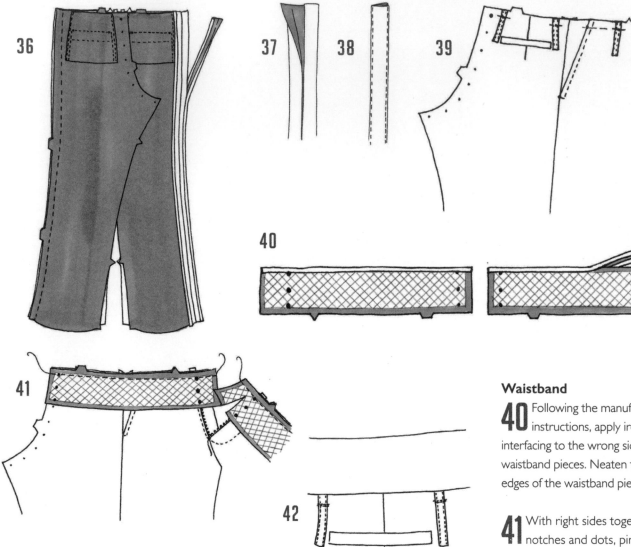

Join back and front pieces

36 With right sides together, pin and stitch the front and back together at the side seams, matching the notches. Press the seams open and neaten the edges with binding.

Belt loops

37 To make belt loops, cut a 19 x 1½in (48 x 4cm) strip of fabric. Turn the long edges in to the centre and press.

38 Fold the strip in half lengthways and stitch along both sides, close to the pressed edges. Cut into six equal lengths of around 3⅛in (8cm).

39 On the right side of the trousers, pin one end of each strip to the waist at the small dots, aligning the raw edges. Tack the strips in place.

Waistband

40 Following the manufacturer's instructions, apply iron-on interfacing to the wrong side of the waistband pieces. Neaten the unnotched edges of the waistband pieces with binding.

41 With right sides together, matching notches and dots, pin and stitch the waistband pieces to the top edge of the trousers, securing the belt loops at the same time. Trim 1½in (4cm) from the front end of the left waistband. Trim the excess zip. Trim and layer the seams. Press the seams towards the waistband.

42 Anchor the belt loops to the trousers by working a line of stitches across each one, ⅜in (1cm) from the waistband seam line. Work a second line of stitching over the first.

Join inside leg and crotch seam

43 With right sides together, matching notches, pin and stitch the front and back of the trouser legs together at the inside leg seams. Press the seams open and neaten the edges with binding.

44 With right sides together, matching the seams, notches and dots, pin and stitch the crotch seam from the end of the stitching at the base of the fly opening at the front, through the centre back and the waistband. Work a second row of stitches over the first to reinforce the seam. Trim the seam between the medium dots. Neaten the edges with binding. Press the back seam open above the medium dot.

45 Turn under and press ½in (1.25cm) at the front edges of the bound edge of the waistband. With right sides together, fold the waistband along the line indicated on the pattern and stitch the front ends. This will hold the bound edges of the waistband away from the fastening when it is turned right side out. Trim the seams.

46 Turn the waistband right side out and press. Pin and tack the waistband in place on the inside of the trousers. On the outside of the garment, stitch along the seam line to secure the waistband on the inside of the garment. Remove the tacking stitches.

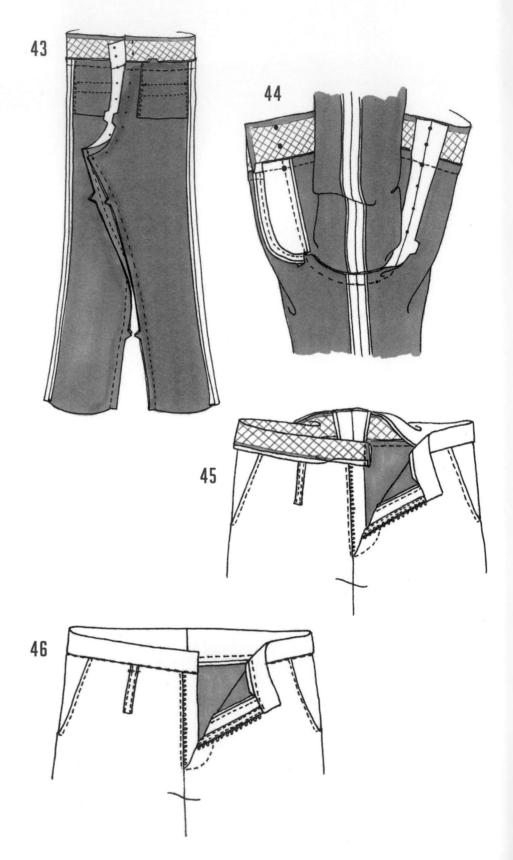

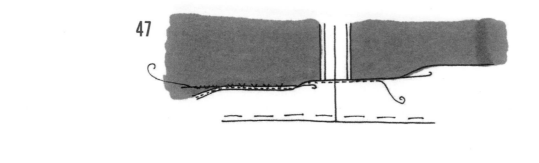

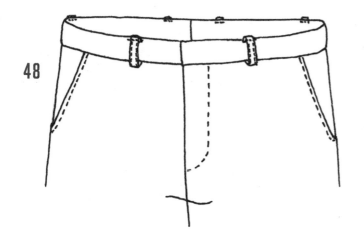

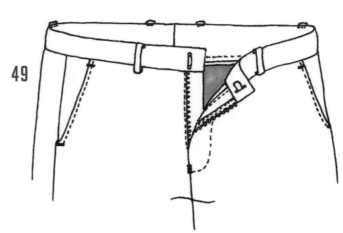

Hem

47 Neaten the raw edge with zigzag stitch, seam binding or by turning under ¼in (0.6cm) and stitching close to the fold. Turn under the hem allowance and tack in place, close to the fold of the hem. Slipstitch the hem by hand (see page 154). Remove the tacking stitches.

Finish belt loops and fastening

48 Turn under ¼in (0.6cm) at the top end of each belt loop. Stitch each one to the top of the waistband, stitching close to the turned edge of each belt loop. Work a second row of stitches over the first to secure the loops.

49 Sew a hook and bar to the waistband to fasten the trousers (see page 171). Work a bar tack by hand or machine (see page 170) at the base of the fly opening, the base of the front pockets and at the top of the front pockets, ⅜in (1cm) from the waistband seam line, taking care not to catch the bound edge of the waistband in the stitches.

PATTERN PIECES

From pattern sheets A, B, C, D, E and F:

27 Back (cut 2 in main fabric)

28 Side (cut 2 in main fabric)

29 Front (cut 2 in main fabric, cut 2 in interfacing)

30 Front facing (cut 2 in main fabric, cut 2 in interfacing)

31 Lower pocket facing (cut 2 in main fabric, cut 2 in interfacing)

32 Breast pocket facing (cut 1 in main fabric)

33 Breast pocket welt (cut 1 in main fabric, cut 1 in interfacing)

34 Lower pocket flap (cut 2 in main fabric, cut 2 in lining fabric, cut 2 in interfacing)

35 Under collar (cut 2 in main fabric, cut 2 in interfacing)

36 Upper sleeve (cut 2 in main fabric)

37 Under sleeve (cut 2 in main fabric)

38 Top collar (cut 1 in main fabric)

39 Breast pocket (cut 2 in lining fabric)

40 Back lining (cut 2 in lining fabric)

41 Under sleeve lining (cut 2 in lining fabric)

42 Front lining (cut 2 in lining fabric)

43 Lower pocket (cut 4 in lining fabric, cut 2 in interfacing)

44 Upper sleeve lining (cut 2 in lining fabric)

45 Side lining (cut 2 in lining fabric)

46 Inside pocket (cut 2 in lining fabric)

JACKET

This lined jacket features plenty of classic details including a notched collar, two inside pockets and two side-back vents. It involves just a small amount of hand sewing as the hems are stitched by machine.

FABRIC REQUIRED

Refer to the appropriate column for your clothing size and the fabric width.

FABRIC WIDTH (WITHOUT NAP)	SMALL	MEDIUM	LARGE
36in (90cm)			
Main fabric:	3 ⅞yd (3.5m)	3 ⅞yd (3.5m)	4yd (3.6m)
Lining fabric:	3⅛yd (2.9m)	3⅛yd (2.9m)	3¼yd (3m)
45in (115cm)			
Main fabric:	2⅝yd (2.4m)	2¾yd (2.5m)	2¾yd (2.5m)
Lining fabric:	2⅝yd (2.4m)	2⅝yd (2.4m)	2¾yd (2.5m)
60in (150cm)			
Main fabric:	2½yd (2.3m)	2½yd (2.3m)	2½yd (2.3m)
Lining fabric:	2yd (1.8m)	2⅛yd (1.9m)	2⅛yd (1.9m)
36in (90cm) medium-weight woven iron-on interfacing	1⅝yd (1.5m)	1¾yd (1.6m)	1¾yd (1.6m)

SUGGESTED FABRICS

For main fabric: Linen, denim, twill, tweed, corduroy, light- to medium-weight wool suiting

For lining: Cotton shirting, cotton mix, viscose, silk, satin, polyester

SEWING NOTIONS

Thread to match the fabric

2 buttons, ¾in (2cm) in diameter

4 buttons, ⅝in (1.5cm) in diameter

1 pair shoulder pads (D-shaped, set-in style)

SEAM ALLOWANCES

Take ⅝in (1.5cm) seam allowances throughout, unless otherwise stated

FINISHED MEASUREMENTS

Finished back length

S: 29½in (75cm)

M: 30in (76cm)

L: 30½in (77.5cm)

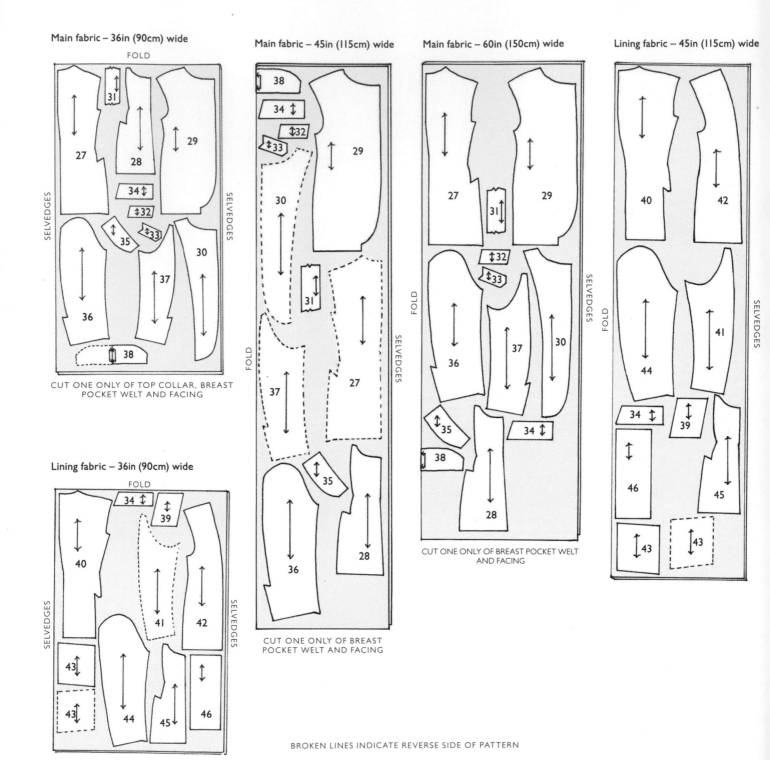

Main fabric – 36in (90cm) wide

CUT ONE ONLY OF TOP COLLAR, BREAST
POCKET WELT AND FACING

Main fabric – 45in (115cm) wide

CUT ONE ONLY OF BREAST
POCKET WELT AND FACING

Main fabric – 60in (150cm) wide

CUT ONE ONLY OF BREAST POCKET WELT
AND FACING

Lining fabric – 45in (115cm) wide

Lining fabric – 36in (90cm) wide

BROKEN LINES INDICATE REVERSE SIDE OF PATTERN

Lining fabric – 60in (150cm) wide

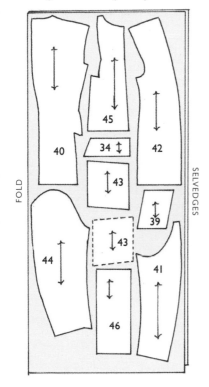

Interfacing – 36in (90cm) wide

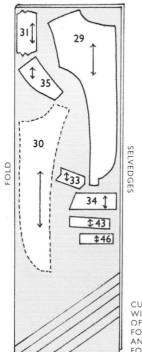

CUT 1½IN (4CM)
WIDE BIAS STRIPS
OF INTERFACING
FOR JACKET HEM
AND VENTS, AND
FOR SLEEVE HEMS

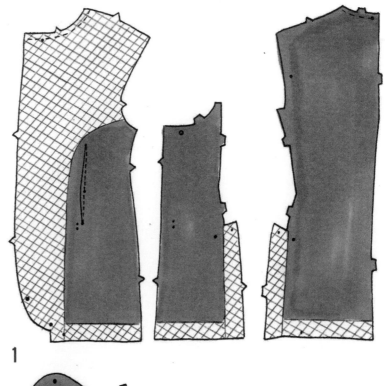

1

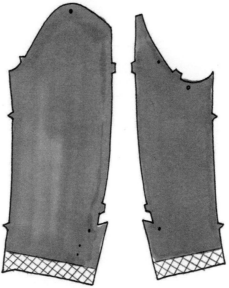

RIGHT SIDE OF FABRIC   WRONG SIDE OF FABRIC   INTERFACING

Front and sides

1 Staystitch (see page 156) the neck edges of the front and back pieces to prevent the fabric from stretching. Stitch the darts on the front pieces (see page 161). Press the darts towards the centre front. Following the manufacturer's instructions, apply iron-on interfacing to the wrong side of each front. Apply 1½in (4cm) wide bias strips of interfacing to the hems of the front, side, back and sleeve pieces, and to the vent extensions on the back and side pieces. Trim the excess interfacing.

Breast pocket

2 Stitch along the breast pocket lines on the left front, between the small dots, to reinforce the opening.

3 Apply interfacing to the wrong side of the welt. With right sides together, fold the welt along the line indicated on the pattern and stitch the short ends along the ¼in (0.6cm) seam line.

4 Turn the welt right side out and press. Tack the raw edges together on each welt.

5 On the outside of the left front, tack the welt to the lower stitching line of the pocket, matching the dots.

6 Press under ¼in (0.6cm) on the long, straight edge of the pocket facing. Pin the wrong side of the facing to the right side of the pocket, aligning the raw edges. Stitch close to the pressed edge of the facing. Tack the raw edges together.

7 With right sides together, pin the unfaced pocket piece to the front, on top of the welt, matching the dots. The ends of the top line taper slightly, so they will not show when the welt is pressed up. Stitch along the stitching lines, between the small dots. Slash the pocket and front on the line indicated on the pattern to within ⅜in (1cm) of both ends. Snip diagonally into the corners, taking care not to cut through the stitches.

8 Draw the pocket piece through the slash to the wrong side of the left front and press. With right sides together, matching the notches and raw edges, stitch the outer edges of the pocket pieces together, catching the triangles at each end of the opening in the stitching.

9 On the outside of the garment, press the welt up, matching the medium dots. Sew the sides of the welt to the front, stitching close to the edges.

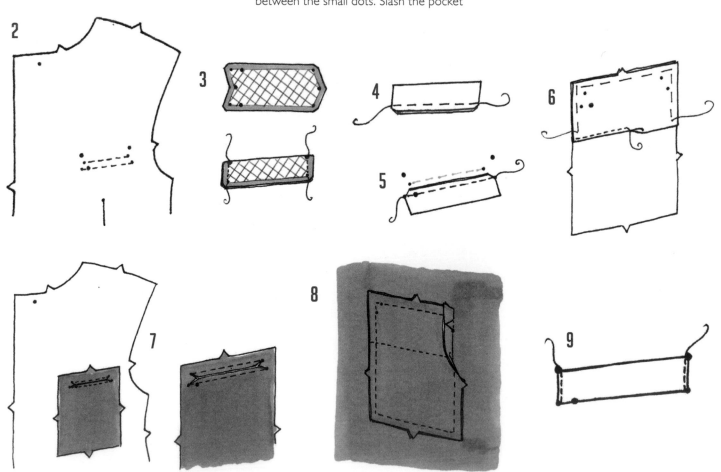

Flaps and lower pockets

10 With right sides together, matching notches, pin and stitch the sides to the fronts. Snip the curves (see page 158). Press the seams open. Following the manufacturer's instructions, apply iron-on interfacing over the pocket lines on the wrong side of the fronts and pocket facings.

11 With wrong sides together, matching the dots, pin one pocket section to each front. Stitch along the stitching lines, between the outer small dots.

12 Turn under and press ¼in (0.6cm) on the lower edge of the facing pieces. Stitch close to the pressed edges. With right sides together, pin the pocket facing to the fronts, matching the dots. Stitch along the stitching lines, between the outer small dots. Do not stitch across the ends. Slash through all layers along the line indicated on the pattern to within ⅜in (1cm) of both ends. Snip diagonally into the corners, taking care not to cut through the stitches.

13 Draw the facing through the slash to the wrong side of the garment. Press the raw edges away from the pocket opening. Fold and press the edges to meet in the centre of the opening, forming an even binding on each side. Stitch the triangular ends on each side of the opening to the ends of the binding.

14 On the outside of the garment, stitch along the edges of the binding, sinking the stitches in the seam line.

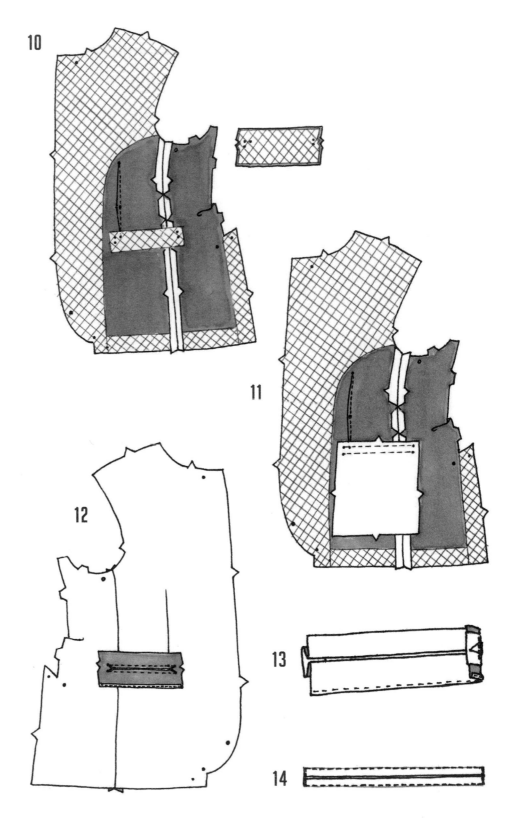

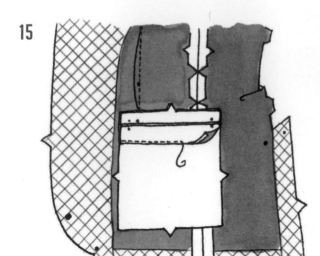

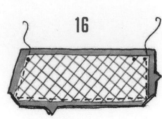

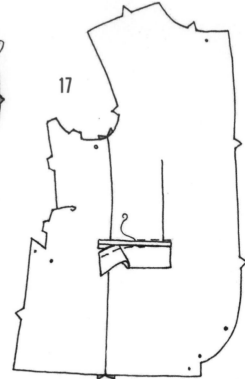

15 On the inside of the garment, fold the pocket away from the garment and stitch the pressed edge of the binding to the pocket piece.

16 Apply interfacing to the wrong side of the two pocket flap lining pieces. With right sides together, stitch the pocket flap linings to the main fabric pieces around the outer edges. Trim the seams and cut diagonally across the corners, taking care not to cut into the stitching (see page 158).

17 Turn right side out and press. Tack the raw edges together. On the outside of the garment, slip the raw edges of the flap through the pocket opening and tack in place.

18 With right sides together, matching the notches and dots, stitch the remaining pocket section to the pocket, joining the pocket flap and catching the clipped corners and ends of binding in the stitching.

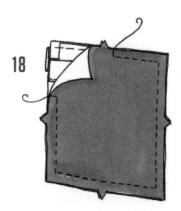

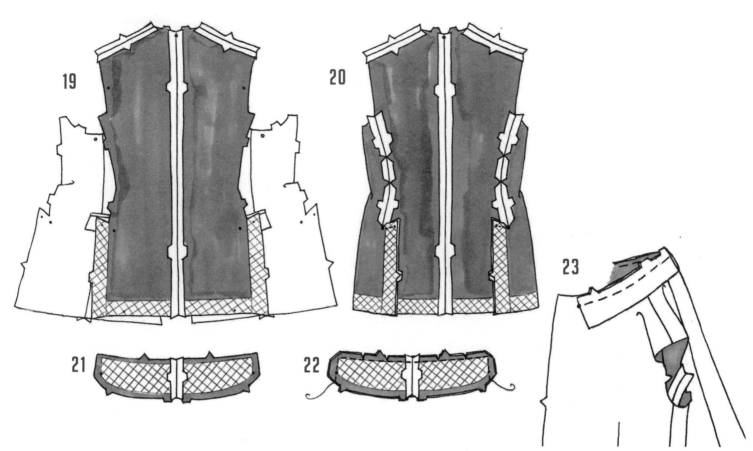

Join back to fronts

19 With right sides together, matching the notches, pin and stitch the centre back seam. Press the seam open. With rights sides together, matching notches, pin and stitch the back to the front pieces at the shoulder seams. Press the seams open.

20 With right sides together, matching the notches and dots, pin and stitch the back to the sides, pivoting the needle at the medium dot and stitching the tops of the vents together, finishing at the small dot. Snip the curves (see page 158). Snip the corner to the medium dot on the side pieces only. Press the seams open above the medium dot.

Collar

21 Following the manufacturer's instructions, apply iron-on interfacing to the wrong side of the under collar pieces. With right sides together, matching notches, pin and stitch the under collar pieces together at the centre back. Press the seam open.

22 With right sides together, matching notches and the medium dots, pin the top collar to the under collar, easing the top collar to fit. Stitch around the outer edges, leaving the neck edge open. Trim the seams, notch the curves and cut diagonally across the corners, taking care not to cut into the stitching.

23 Turn right side out and press, rolling the seam towards the under collar and aligning the raw edges. Tack the raw edges of the collar together. With the right side of the under collar to the right side of the jacket, pin and tack the collar to the neck edge, matching the notches and dots.

Sleeves

24 Pin and stitch the back seam of the under and upper sleeve together, matching the notches, pivoting the needle at the medium dot and finishing within ¼in (0.6cm) of the raw edge. Snip the under sleeve to the small dot. Press the seam open above the small dot.

25 Run two rows of gathering stitches (see page 162) in between the notches, by hand or using a long machine stitch, working one row along the seam line and the other ¼in (0.6cm) inside the seam line, to ease the fullness of the top of the sleeve. Pin and stitch the front seam of the under and upper sleeve together, matching the notches. Press the seam open.

26 Turn the hem allowance to the outside of the sleeve. Stitch the edges of the hem to the vent extensions, allowing ¼in (0.6cm) seams.

27 Turn the hem to the inside. Turn the upper sleeve extension to the inside to form a facing and slipstitch (see page 154) the side and lower edges to the hem allowance.

28 On the outside, lap the upper sleeve opening over the under sleeve extension and tack together.

29 With right sides together, pin the sleeve to the armhole, matching the notches and underarm dots, the large dot at the shoulder, the back side seam to the small dot and the back sleeve seam to the medium dot. Pull up the gathering stitches to fit, adjusting them so they are evenly distributed. Insert plenty of pins to help ease the fullness of the sleeve head. Stitch the sleeve into the armhole. Work a second line of stitches close to the first to reinforce the seam. Trim the seam below the notches. Press the seam towards the sleeve.

30 Fold the shoulder pads in half and mark the centre with a pin or tacking stitches. Pin the shoulder pads in place, matching the centre of the pad with the shoulder seam and aligning the straight edge of the pad with the edge of the armhole seam allowance. Stitch the shoulder pads to the seam allowances of the armhole and shoulder seams.

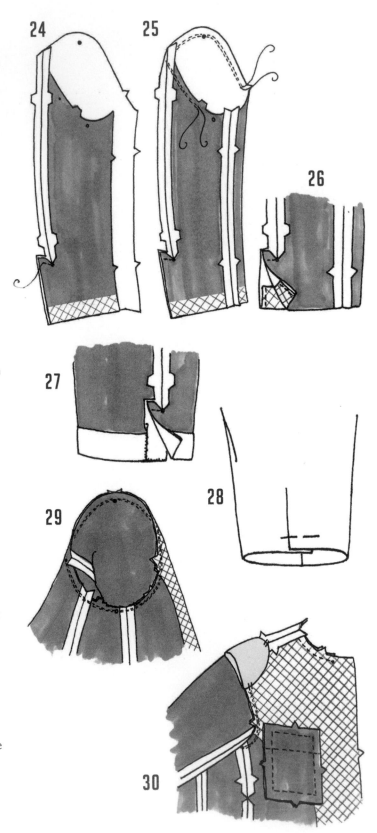

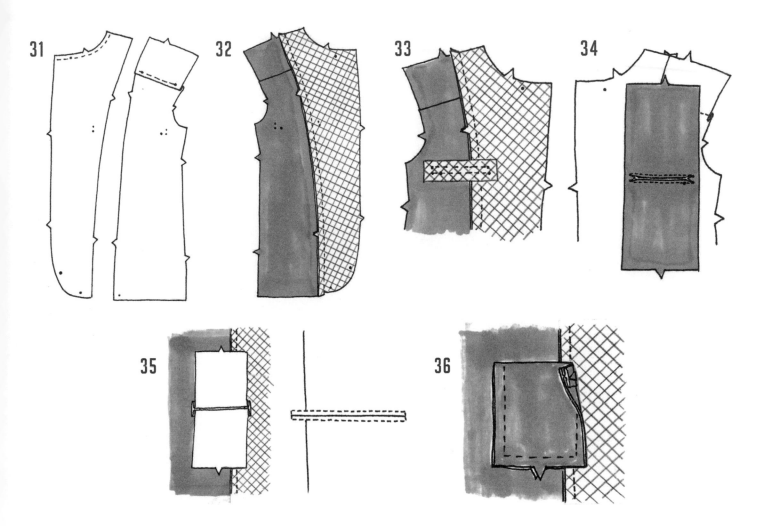

Facings and front lining

31 Staystitch the neck edges of the front facings to prevent the fabric from stretching. To make the pleat in the front lining, fold the fabric with wrong sides together, matching the dots. Tack along the broken lines indicated on the pattern. Press the pleat towards the hem.

32 Following the manufacturer's instructions, apply iron-on interfacing to the wrong side of the left and right front facings. With right sides together, pin and stitch the front linings to the front facings, matching the notches and dots. Press the seam towards the lining.

Inside pockets

33 Apply interfacing over the pocket lines on the wrong side of the front lining pieces. Stitch along the pocket lines on the front linings and facings, between the small dots, to reinforce the openings.

34 With right sides together, pin the pocket piece to the front lining, matching the dots. Stitch along the stitching lines. Slash the pocket, lining and facing on the line indicated on the pattern to within ⅜in (1cm) of both ends. Snip diagonally into the corners, taking care not to cut through the stitches.

35 Draw the pocket through the slash to the wrong side of the lining. Fold and press the edges to meet in the centre of the opening, forming an even binding on each side. On the outside of the garment, stitch around the opening, sinking the stitches in the seam line, to secure the binding.

36 With right sides together, press the upper section of the pocket over the lower section. Stitch the outer edges of the pocket together, catching the triangular pieces down in the stitching.

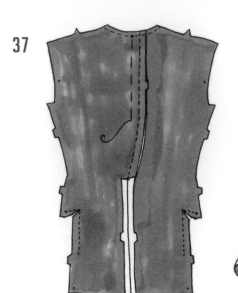

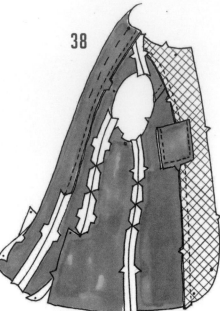

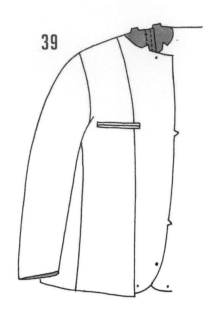

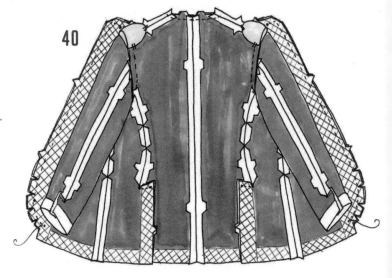

Back lining

37 Staystitch the neck edges of the back lining pieces. With right sides together, matching the notches, pin and stitch the centre back seam. To form the pleat in the back, with right sides together, tack along the broken line indicated on the pattern. Snip the centre back seam to the medium dot. Press the seam open below the snip. Press the pleat to one side. Reinforce the corners at the back vents with a row of stitches along the seam line from the medium dot, pivoting the needle at the small dot and stitching towards the hem, finishing at the notch. Snip to the small dot.

Join lining pieces

38 With right sides together, matching notches, pin and stitch the side to the front linings. With right sides together, matching notches, pin and stitch the back to the front pieces at the shoulder seams. With right sides together, matching the notches and dots, pin and stitch the back to the sides, finishing at the medium dot. Snip the curves (see page 158). Snip the corner to the medium dot on the side pieces. Press the seams open.

Sleeve linings

39 Pin and stitch the back seam of the under and upper sleeve together, matching the notches. Press the seam open. Follow steps 24–25 and step 29 to complete the sleeves and set them into the jacket lining.

Attach lining to jacket

40 With right sides of jacket and lining together, matching the seams and pattern markings, pin and stitch the front and neck edges together between the medium dots, leaving the hem loose. Trim the seam, clip the curves and cut diagonally across the corners, taking care not to cut through the stitches.

Vents

41 With right sides together, matching notches and dots, pin and stitch the side vents to the side vent linings, starting at the small dot and ending around 4in (10cm) above the hem edge. Pin and stitch the back vents to the back vent linings, with right sides together, matching notches and dots, starting at the small dot and ending around 4in (10cm) above the hem edge.

42 With right sides together, matching notches and dots, pin and stitch the top of the vent linings together, between the small and medium dots.

Hem

43 With right sides together, align the lower edge of the back lining with the edge of the jacket, matching the small dots and centre back seams. Pin and stitch in place along the seam line, between the small dots.

44 With right sides together, align the lower edge of the front and side linings with the edge of the jacket, matching the seams. Pin and stitch in place along the seam line, starting at the seam allowance of the side edge and ending at the small dot on the front.

45 With right sides together, turn up the hem and stitch to the seam allowances of the side vent edges of the jacket. Turn under the seam allowance at each side of the back hem. With right sides together, turn up the hem at the back vents and stitch along the 1½in (4cm) hem allowances.

46 With right sides together, insert the sleeve with the turned-up hem into the sleeve lining, matching the front seams and aligning the back seam of the lining with the edge of the opening of the upper sleeve. Make sure that neither the sleeve nor the lining are twisted. Pin and stitch the sleeve and lining together each side of the opening.

47 Secure the jacket and sleeve hems to the seam allowances with a few hand stitches.

48 Stitch the top of the underlap and overlap of the vent together at the seam, sewing through all layers of lining and main fabric to hold the vent in place.

49 To turn the work right side out, carefully unpick around 7in (18cm) on a seam of the sleeve lining. This will provide you with a pressed seam, making it easier to stitch closed. Pull the jacket to the right side through the opening in the sleeve lining. To close the opening in the sleeve lining, with wrong sides together, pin and stitch close to the pressed edges on the right side. Take care not to catch the main sleeve fabric in the stitches.

50 Press the jacket. Slipstitch the opening at the edges where the front facings and hem meet. Lay the extra length of lining in a downward fold and slipstitch the openings to the vent edges.

51 Slipstitch the gaps in the lining at the sleeve openings.

52 Remove the tacking stitches. Finish by working two buttonholes by hand or machine (see page 168) on the left front, as indicated on the pattern. Lap the left front over the right front of the jacket, matching the centres. Mark the position of buttons to correspond with the buttonholes. Attach the buttons to the right front (see page 169). Sew two buttons to each sleeve at the small dots, stitching through all layers.

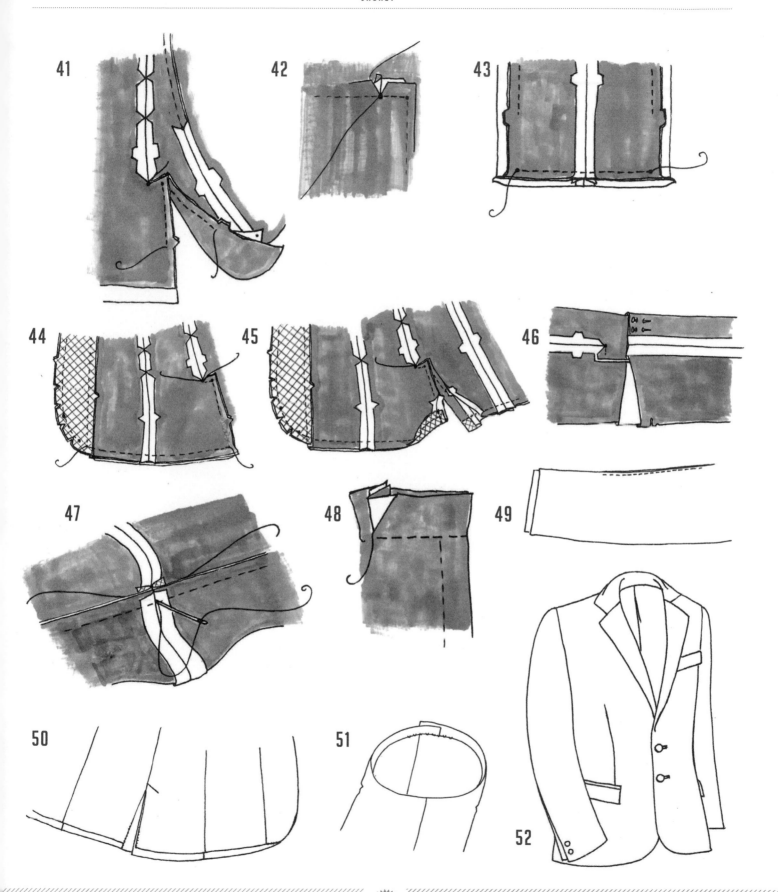

BOXER SHORTS

Flat-fell seams are used for a neat and durable finish on these classic boxer shorts. They feature an elasticated waistband in a contrasting fabric and there is a single button to fasten the fly.

PATTERN PIECES

From pattern sheet E:

47 Waistband (cut 2)
48 Fly facing (cut 1)
49 Front and back (cut 2)

FABRIC REQUIRED

Refer to the appropriate column for your clothing size and the fabric width.

FABRIC WIDTH (WITHOUT NAP)	SMALL	MEDIUM	LARGE
36in (90cm)	1¼yd (1.1m)	1⅓yd (1.2m)	1⅓yd (1.2m)
45in (115cm)	1¼yd (1.1m)	1⅓yd (1.2m)	1⅓yd (1.2m)
60in (150cm)	⅝yd (0.6m)	1⅓yd (1.2m)	1⅓yd (1.2m)
FOR WAISTBAND			
36in (90cm)	⅛yd (0.1m)	¼yd (0.2m)	¼yd (0.2m)
45in (115cm)	¼yd (0.2m)	¼yd (0.2m)	¼yd (0.2m)
60in (150cm)	⅛yd (0.1m)	⅛yd (0.1m)	⅛yd (0.1m)

SUGGESTED FABRICS

Cotton, cotton shirting, chambray

SEWING NOTIONS

Thread to match the fabric
1in (2.5cm) wide elastic to fit the waist comfortably
Bodkin or safety pin
1 button, ⅜in (1cm) in diameter

SEAM ALLOWANCES

Take ⅝in (1.5cm) seam allowances throughout, unless otherwise stated

FINISHED MEASUREMENTS

Finished back length
S: 14⅛in (36cm)
M: 14¾in (37.5cm)
L: 15⅜in (39cm)

PATTERN NOTE

Construct the boxer shorts with flat-fell seams (see page 160).

36 & 45in (90 & 115cm) wide fabric

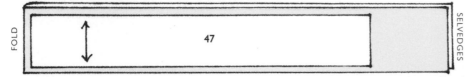

SELVEDGE

47

47

SELVEDGE

60in (150cm) wide fabric

FOLD

47

SELVEDGES

36 & 45in (90 & 115cm) wide fabric for all sizes
60in (150cm) wide fabric for medium & large sizes only

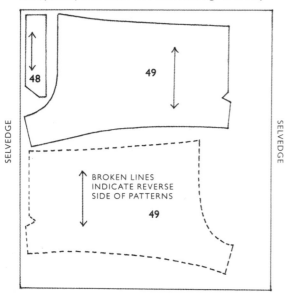

SELVEDGE

48

49

SELVEDGE

BROKEN LINES
INDICATE REVERSE
SIDE OF PATTERNS

49

49

60in (150cm) wide fabric for small size only

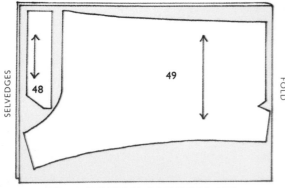

SELVEDGES

48

49

FOLD

OPEN OUT FABRIC TO CUT THE FLY FACING

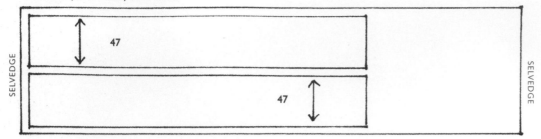

1

2

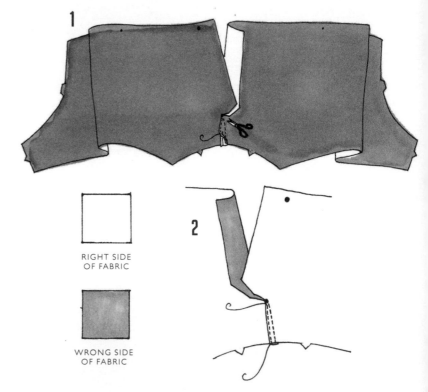

RIGHT SIDE
OF FABRIC

WRONG SIDE
OF FABRIC

1 With right sides together, pin and stitch the centre front seam to the medium dot. Snip to the medium dot. Trim the edge on the left front and finish the flat-fell seam on the inside of the boxer shorts. The rest of the flat-fell seams should be finished on the outside of the shorts.

2 On the outside of the garment, topstitch close to the centre front seam.

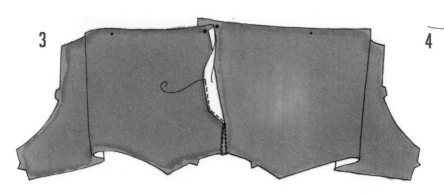

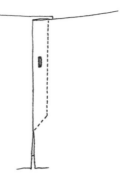

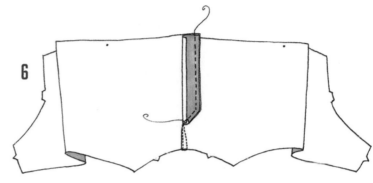

Fly opening

3 Fold under the fly extension of the left front at the line indicated on the pattern. Turn under and press the seam allowance and stitch in place.

4 Work a buttonhole in the left front, as indicated on the pattern.

5 Turn under and press the seam allowance on the long and lower edges of the fly facing.

6 With right sides together, matching the notches, pin and stitch the fly facing to the right front extension. Trim the seam.

7 Turn the fly to the inside and press. Topstitch the long edge in place.

8 On the outside of the garment, lap the left front over the right, matching the large dots. Topstitch the lower end of the fly, sewing through all layers along the broken lines indicated on the pattern from the medium dot, over the previous lines of topstitching, across the fly and then close to the edge of the fold, finishing at the medium dot. Tack the top edges of the fly together.

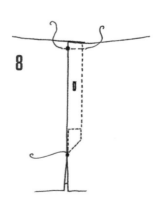

Back and inside leg seams

9 With wrong sides together, matching the notches, pin and stitch the centre back seam of the boxer shorts. Trim the seam at the left back edge and finish the flat-fell seam.

10 With wrong sides together, matching the notches and seams, pin and stitch the inside leg seams together. Trim the seam at the front edge and finish the flat-fell seam.

Waistband

11 With right sides together, stitch the short edges of the waistband pieces together. Press the seams open. Press under the seam allowance on the lower edge of the waistband.

12 With the right side of the waistband to the wrong side of the upper edge of the boxer shorts, matching the seams to the small dots, pin and stitch the waistband to the boxer shorts. Press the waistband up. Press the seam towards the waistband.

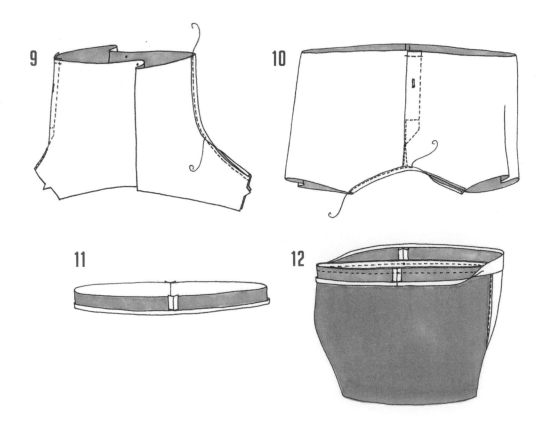

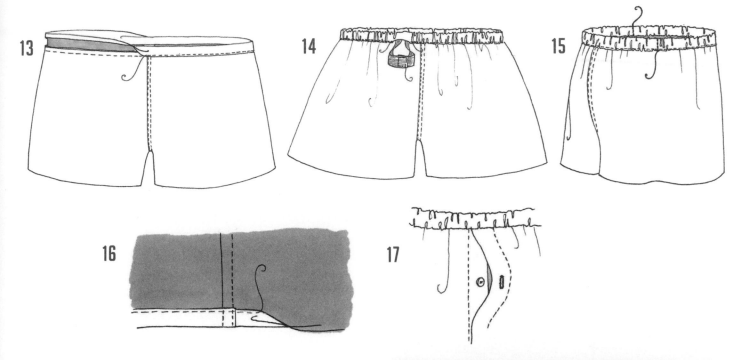

13 On the outside of the garment, pin the pressed edge of the waistband over the seam. Topstitch close to the pressed edge, leaving an opening at the back to insert the elastic.

14 Using a bodkin or a safety pin, insert the elastic through the opening in the waistband. Make sure the elastic does not twist as you pass it through the waistband and back out of the opening. Overlap ¾in (2cm) at the ends of the elastic so it lays flat. Stitch the ends together securely by hand or machine.

15 Push the ends of the elastic into the waistband. Topstitch the opening in the waistband. On the outside of the boxer shorts, run a line of stitches, by hand or machine, along the side seams of the waistband to prevent the elastic from twisting when worn or laundered.

Hem

16 Turn under ¾in (2cm) at the hem of each leg and press. Turn under and press the raw edge. Stitch the hem.

17 Sew a button to the right front to correspond with the buttonhole.

Night Attire

PATTERN PIECES

From pattern sheets A, B, C, D and E:

50 Front (cut 2)
51 Front facing (cut 2 in interfacing)
52 Pocket (cut 1)
53 Collar (cut 2 in main fabric,
     cut 1 in interfacing)
54 Back (cut 1)
55 Back facing (cut 1)
56 Sleeve (cut 2)
57 Trouser (cut 2)
58 Trouser facing (cut 1)

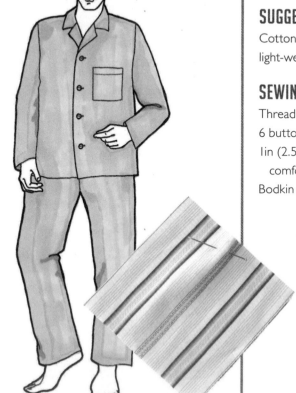

PYJAMAS

Whether made in traditional striped fabric or something more whimsical, these pyjamas will ensure stylish slumber. If using striped fabric, add a twist by cutting the pyjama top pocket so the stripes run horizontally.

FABRIC REQUIRED

Refer to the appropriate column for your clothing size and the fabric width.

FABRIC WIDTH (WITHOUT NAP)	SMALL	MEDIUM	LARGE
36in (90cm)	6½yd (5.9m)	6⅝yd (6m)	6⅝yd (6m)
45in (115cm)	5¼yd (4.8m)	5⅜yd (4.9m)	5⅜yd (4.9m)
60in (150cm)	5yd (4.5m)	5¼yd (4.8m)	5¼yd (4.8m)
36in (90cm) light-weight iron-on interfacing	⅞yd (0.8m)	⅞yd (0.8m)	⅞yd (0.8m)

SUGGESTED FABRICS

Cotton shirting, brushed cotton, light-weight linen, chambray

SEWING NOTIONS

Thread to match the fabric
6 buttons, ⅝in (1.5cm) in diameter
1in (2.5cm) wide elastic to fit the waist
  comfortably
Bodkin or safety pin

SEAM ALLOWANCES

Take ⅝in (1.5cm) seam allowances throughout, unless otherwise stated

FINISHED MEASUREMENTS

Finished back length
S: 27¼in (69.5cm)
M: 27½in (70cm)
L: 27¾in (70.5cm)
Side length of pyjama trousers
S: 41½in (105cm)
M: 41¾in (106cm)
L: 42in (107cm)

36in (90cm) wide fabric

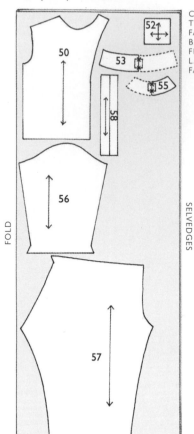

50

53

55

52

58

56

FOLD

SELVEDGES

57

CUT POCKET, TROUSER FACING AND BACK FACING FROM A SINGLE LAYER OF FABRIC

52

45in (115cm) and 60in (150cm) wide fabric

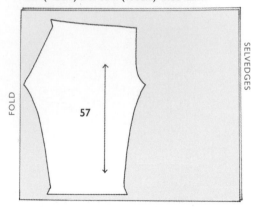

FOLD

57

SELVEDGES

60in (150cm) wide fabric

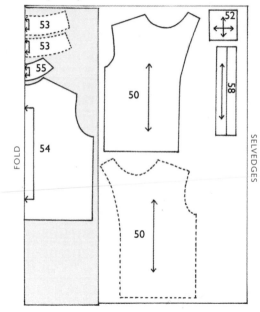

53

53

55

52

58

FOLD

54

50

SELVEDGES

50

45in (115cm) wide fabric

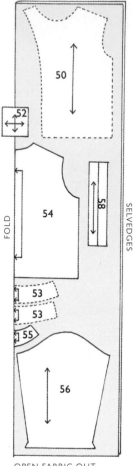

50

52

54

58

FOLD

53

53

55

56

SELVEDGES

OPEN FABRIC OUT TO CUT POCKET AND TROUSER FACING

36in (90cm) wide fabric

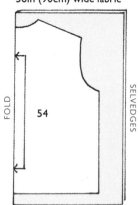

FOLD

54

SELVEDGES

60in (150cm) wide fabric

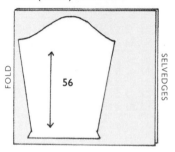

FOLD

56

SELVEDGES

BROKEN LINES INDICATE REVERSE SIDE OF PATTERN

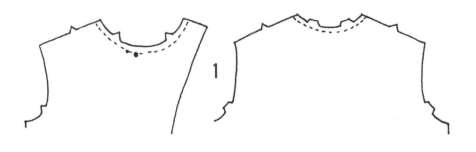

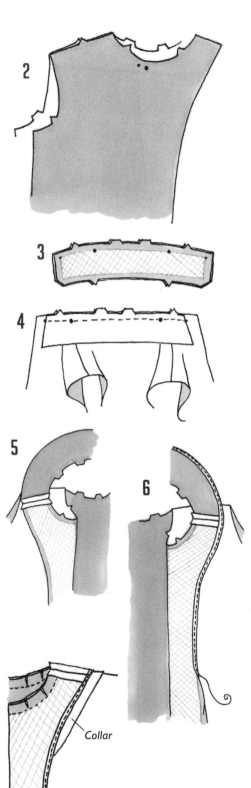

PYJAMA TOP

1 Staystitch (see page 156) the neck edges of the front and back pieces to prevent the fabric from stretching.

Join back to front

2 With right sides together, matching notches, pin and stitch the front pieces to the back at the shoulder seams.

Collar and facings

3 Following the manufacturer's instructions, apply iron-on interfacing to the wrong side of one collar piece. This will be the under collar. With right sides together, pin the second collar piece to the under collar. Stitch around the three outer edges, leaving the neck edge open. Trim the seams and cut diagonally across the corners (see page 158). Turn right side out and press.

4 With the right side of the under collar to the right side of the garment, matching notches, medium dots and small dots to the shoulder seams, pin the neck edges together. Tack the collar in place, stitching through all the layers.

5 Following the manufacturer's instructions, apply iron-on interfacing (see page 145) to the wrong side of the left and right front facings. Stitch the front facings to the back facing at the shoulder edges. Press the seams open.

6 Turn under and press a ¼in (0.6cm) hem around the outside edge of the left and right front facings and the back facing. Stitch close to the pressed-under edges.

7 With right sides together, turn the neck edge of the facings at the fold line as indicated on the pattern piece. Matching the notches and shoulder seams, pin and stitch the facings to the garment at the neck edge. Trim the seam, snip the curves (see page 158) and cut diagonally across the corners, taking care not to cut into the stitches.

RIGHT SIDE OF FABRIC	WRONG SIDE OF FABRIC	INTERFACING

Collar

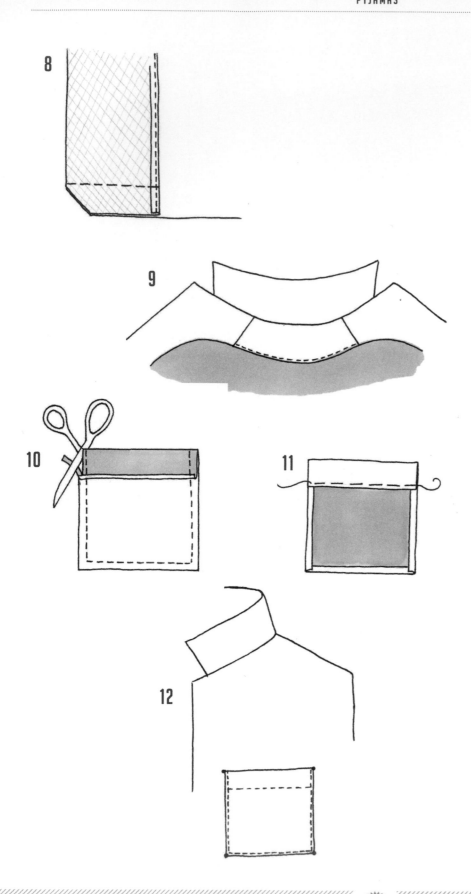

8 With right sides together, turn the lower edges of the facings at the fold line, as indicated on the pattern. Stitch across the lower edge of the front facings, allowing a 1in (2.5cm) hem. Cut diagonally across the corners, taking care not to cut into the stitching.

9 Turn the facings right side out and press. Press the back facing to the inside of the garment. Pin the lower, turned edge of the facing to the pyjama back, then tack and stitch in place in between the shoulder seams, either by hand or by machine.

Pocket

10 Press under ¼in (0.6cm) along the top edge of the pocket. Turn the top edge to the outside of the pocket along the fold line to form the facing. Stitch along the seam line along the side and bottom edges. Trim the seams to ¼in (0.6cm).

11 Turn the facing to the inside. Turn under the raw edges along the stitch line from the previous step and press. Tack the facing down, close to the turned edge. Topstitch (see page 156) along the tacking line, then remove the tacking stitches.

12 Pin the pocket to the outside of the left front, matching the small dots. Stitch close to the side and lower edges.

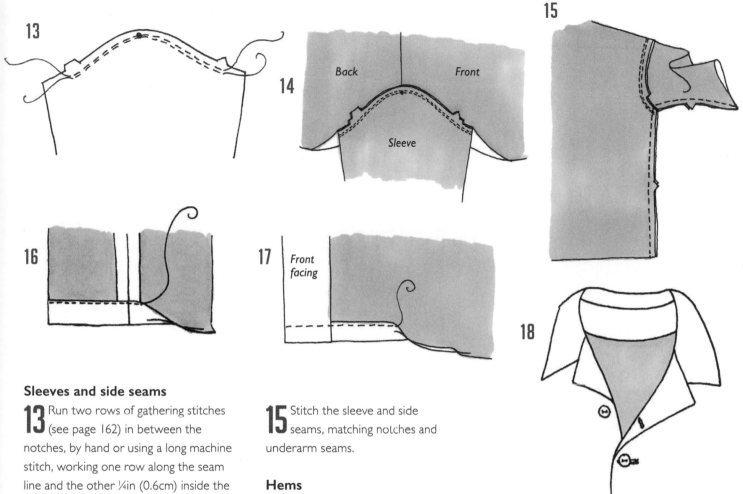

Sleeves and side seams

13 Run two rows of gathering stitches (see page 162) in between the notches, by hand or using a long machine stitch, working one row along the seam line and the other ¼in (0.6cm) inside the seam line, to ease the fullness of the top of the sleeve.

14 With right sides together, pin the sleeve to the armhole, aligning the centre dot with the shoulder seam. Match notches and seam lines at the underarms. Pull up the gathering stitches to fit, adjusting them so they are evenly distributed. Insert plenty of pins to help ease the fullness of the sleeve head. Stitch between the underarm seams and work a second line of stitches close to the first for added strength. Trim each side of the seam allowance separately, from the underarm to the notch. Press the seam towards the sleeve.

15 Stitch the sleeve and side seams, matching notches and underarm seams.

Hems

16 Turn up the sleeve hems and press. Turn under and press ¼in (0.6cm) on the lower edge of the sleeve. Stitch close to the turned raw edges.

17 Turn up the hem and press. Turn under and press ¼in (0.6cm) on the hem, tucking it under behind the front facings. Stitch close to the turned raw edge, working right across the front facings to the end.

Finishing off

18 Finish by working four buttonholes by hand or machine (see page 168) on the left front. Lap the left front over the right, matching the centre front. Mark the position of buttons to correspond with the buttonholes. Attach the buttons to the right front.

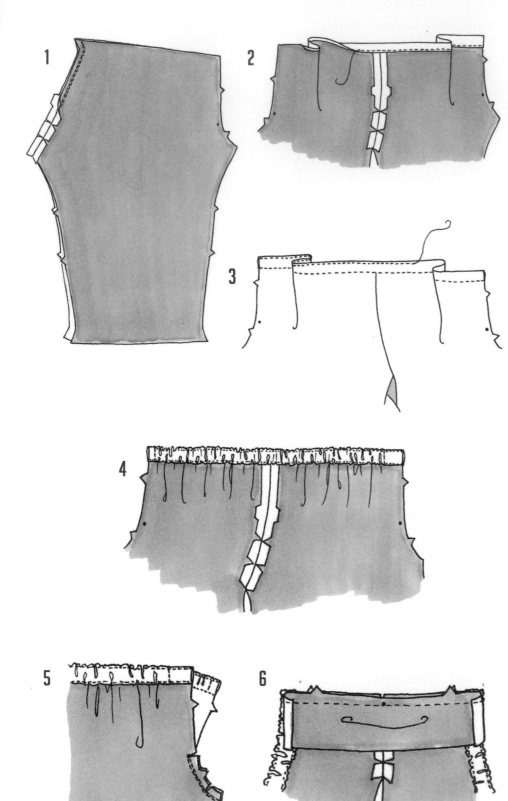

PYJAMA TROUSERS

1 With right sides together, matching the notches, join the centre back seam. Stitch a second row over the first to reinforce the seam. Snip the curves (see page 158) and press the seam open.

Waist

2 Turn and press the top edge of the trousers to the inside along the fold line. Press under ¼in (0.6cm) along the raw edge. Sew in place, close to the turned raw edge.

3 Topstitch close to the top edge of the waist to form a casing for the elastic.

4 Using a bodkin or a safety pin, insert the elastic through the opening in the waistband. Adjust to fit. On the left side of the opening, stitch down the end of the elastic 1½in (4cm) from the seam line. On the right side of the opening, secure the end of the elastic by sewing it down along the seam line. Trim the excess elastic.

Front opening

5 With right sides together, matching the notches, join the centre front seam to the dot. Stitch a second row over the first to reinforce the seam. Snip the curves (see page 158) and snip to the dot. Press the seam open.

6 Press under ⅝in (1.5cm) at the short edges of the facing. With the right side of the trouser facing to the wrong side of the trousers, pin and stitch the facing to the opening. Trim the seam and press towards the facing.

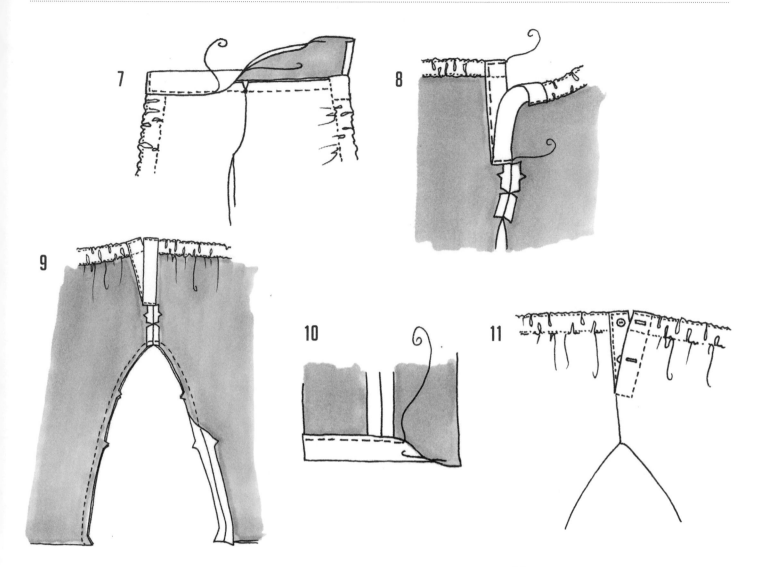

7 Turn under and press ⅝in (1.5cm) on the other side of the facing. Fold the facing along the line indicated on the pattern and pin the long pressed edge of the facing over the seam. Topstitch (see page 156) close to the pressed edges over the seam and at the top of the waist.

8 Turn the facing on the left side of the opening to the inside, leaving the facing on the right side of the opening on the outside of the garment. Tack in place at the top of the waist, down the side and across the lower edge. On the right side of the trousers, topstitch, following the line of tacking. Remove the tacking stitches.

Inside leg seams

9 With right sides together, matching the notches and seams, stitch the inside leg seams. Press the seams open.

Hem

10 Turn under 1in (2.5cm) at the hem of each leg and press. Turn the raw edge under and press, then stitch the hem.

11 Work two buttonholes (see page 168) at the left front opening, as indicated on the pattern. Sew buttons to the right front to correspond with the buttonholes.

DRESSING GOWN

Featuring a shawl collar, two large patch pockets, a tie belt and shaped, turn-back cuffs, this garment can be made in a warm woollen fabric for the cold season and in a cool cotton shirting for lounging in warm weather.

PATTERN PIECES

From pattern sheets B, C, D, E and F:

59 Cuff (cut 4 in main fabric, cut 2 in interfacing)
60 Under sleeve (cut 2 in main fabric)
61 Front (cut 2 in main fabric)
62 Lower front facing (cut 2 in main fabric, cut 2 in interfacing)
63 Belt (cut 2 in main fabric)
64 Upper front facing (cut 1 in main fabric, cut 1 in interfacing)
65 Back (cut 1 in main fabric)
66 Pocket (cut 2 in main fabric)
67 Top sleeve (cut 2 in main fabric)

FABRIC REQUIRED

Refer to the appropriate column for your clothing size and the fabric width.

FABRIC WIDTH (WITHOUT NAP)	SMALL	MEDIUM	LARGE
54in (137cm)	4yd (3.6m)	4⅛yd (3.7m)	4¼yd (3.8m)
60in (150cm)	3¼yd (3m)	3⅜yd (3.1m)	3½yd (3.2m)
36in (90cm) light- to medium-weight iron-on interfacing	Non-woven 1¾yd (1.6m)	Non-woven 1¾yd (1.6m)	Non-woven 1¾yd (1.6m)
	Woven 2yd (1.8m)	Woven 2yd (1.8m)	Woven 2⅛yd (1.9m)

SUGGESTED FABRICS

Cotton shirting, silk, linen, flannel, wool, wool mix

SEWING NOTIONS

Thread to match the fabric

SEAM ALLOWANCES

Take ⅝in (1.5cm) seam allowances throughout, unless otherwise stated

FINISHED MEASUREMENTS

Finished back length
S: 50⅝in (128.5cm)
M: 51⅜in (130.5cm)
L: 52⅜in (133cm)

54in (137cm) wide fabric

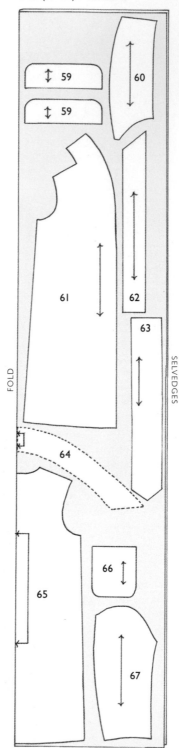

60in (150cm) wide fabric

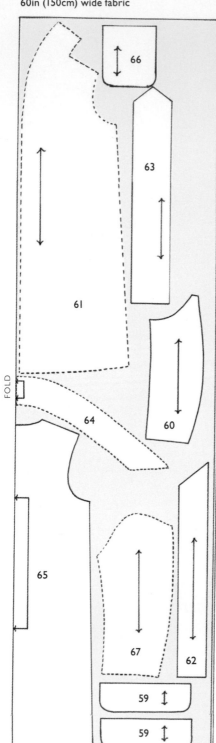

Non-woven interfacing

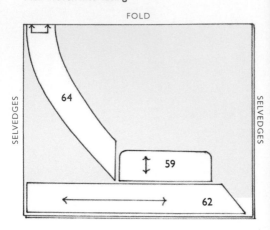

Woven interfacing

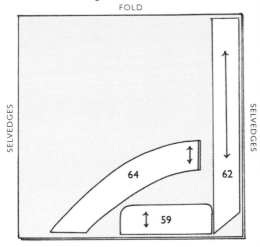

ADD ¼IN (0.6CM) WHEN CUTTING OUT THE
CENTRE BACK OF THE UPPER FRONT INTERFACING.
OVERLAP THE ENDS AT THE CENTRE BACK WHEN
APPLYING THE INTERFACING TO THE FABRIC

BROKEN LINES INDICATE REVERSE SIDE OF PATTERN

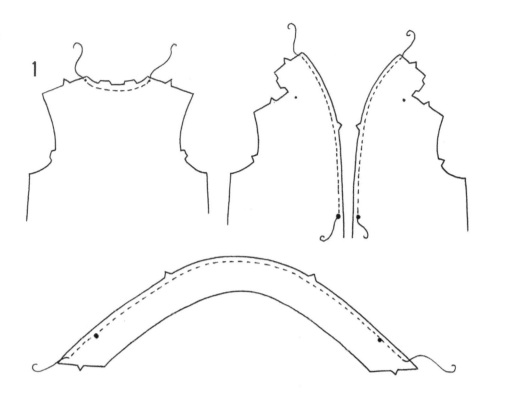

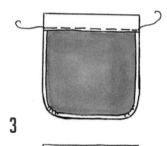

1 Staystitch (see page 156) around the neck edge of the back, the curved edges of the front pieces to the large dot and the outer edges of the upper front facing to prevent the fabric from stretching.

RIGHT SIDE
OF FABRIC

Pockets

2 Turn under and press ¼in (0.6cm) along the top edge of the pocket. Turn the top of the pocket to the outside along the fold line to form the facing. Stitch along the ⅝in (1.5cm) seam line of the side and lower edges. Trim the seams of the side and lower edges to ¼in (0.6cm).

WRONG SIDE
OF FABRIC

3 Turn the facing to the inside. Turn under the raw edges along the stitch line from the previous step and press. Tack the facing down, close to the pressed edge. Topstitch along the tacking line, then remove the tacking stitches.

INTERFACING

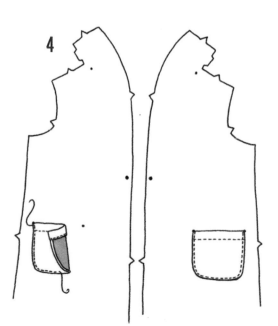

4 Pin a pocket to the outside of each front piece, matching small dots. Tack in position and stitch close to the side and lower edges.

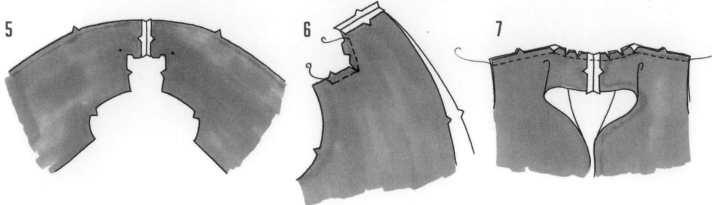

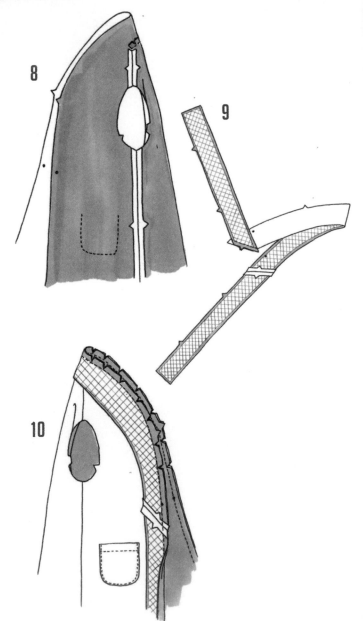

Join back and front pieces

5 With right sides together, matching notches, stitch the centre back seam of the collar. Press open.

6 Reinforce the corners at the neck and shoulder of the front pieces with a row of stitches along the seam line, between the notches. Snip to the medium dot.

7 With right sides together, matching notches and dots, pin and stitch the front pieces to the back at the neck and shoulder seams, easing in the fullness of the back at the shoulders. Snip the seam at the neck. Press the neck seam towards the collar. Press the shoulder seams open.

Side seams

8 With right sides together, stitch the side seams, matching notches and underarm seams. Press the seams open.

Front facings

9 Following the manufacturer's instructions, apply iron-on interfacing to the wrong side of the upper and lower front facing pieces. If using woven interfacing, overlap the separate interfacing pieces (see cutting layout) at the centre back when applying them to the wrong side of the upper front facing. With right sides together, matching notches, pin and stitch the upper and lower front facing pieces together. Press the seams open.

10 With right sides together, matching notches and dots, pin and stitch the front facing to the garment. Trim the seam and notch the curves. Press the seam towards the facing.

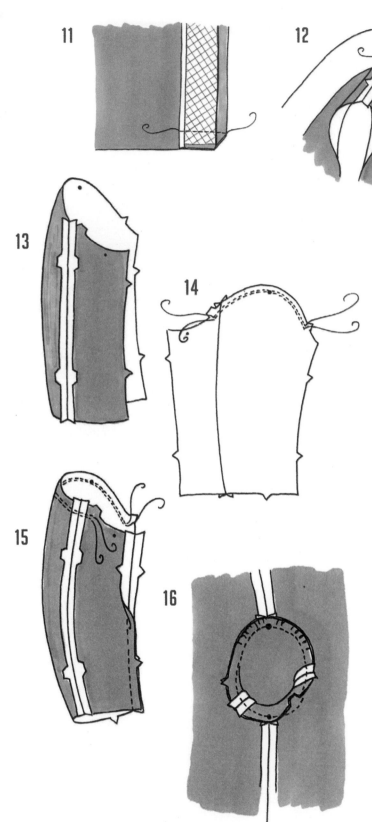

11 Turn under and press ¼in (0.6cm) on the raw edges of the facings. With right sides together, stitch across the lower edge of the front facings, allowing a 1½in (4cm) hem. Cut diagonally across the corners, taking care not to cut the stitching.

12 Turn the facing to the inside of the garment. Stitch the pressed edge of the facing over the back neck seam, between the shoulder seams.

Sleeves

13 Pin and stitch the back seam of the under and upper sleeve together, matching the notches and easing the fullness. Press the seam open.

14 Run two rows of gathering stitches (see page 162) in between the notches, by hand or using a long machine stitch, working one row along the seam line and the other ¼in (0.6cm) inside the seam line, to ease the fullness of the top of the sleeve.

15 Pin and stitch the front seam of the under and upper sleeve together, matching the notches. Press the seam open.

16 With right sides together, pin the sleeve to the armhole, matching the notches, the large dot at the shoulder and the medium dot to the underarm seam. Pull up the gathering stitches to fit, adjusting them so they are evenly distributed. Insert plenty of pins to help ease the fullness of the sleeve head. Stitch the sleeve into the armhole. Press the seam towards the sleeve.

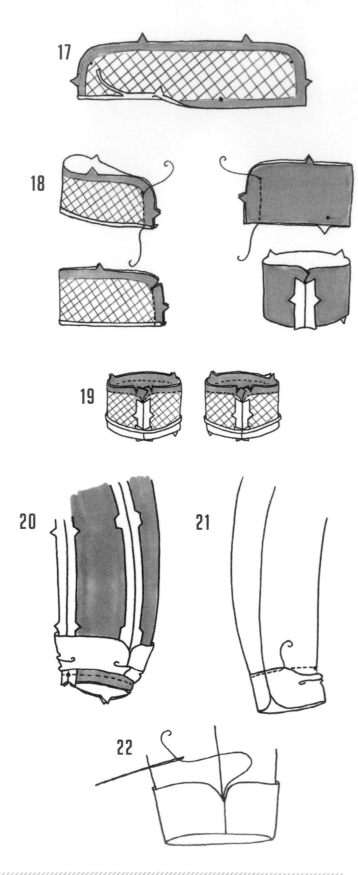

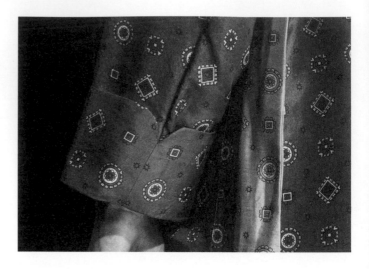

Cuffs

17 Following the manufacturer's instructions, apply iron-on interfacing (see page 145) to the wrong side of one cuff piece. This will be the cuff facing. Press under ⅝in (1.5cm) along the long, lower straight edge of the cuff facing. Trim to ¼in (0.6cm).

18 Sew the ends together of both the cuff and cuff facing, from the small dot to the lower edges. Snip to the dot and press the seams open.

19 With right sides together, matching the notches and shaping, pin the cuff to the cuff facing. Stitch the top edges together between the dots. Trim the seam and notch the curves.

20 Turn the cuff right side out and press. With the right side of the cuff to the wrong side of the sleeve, pin and stitch together, matching the notches, the medium dot to the front sleeve seam, and the cuff seam to the seam at the back of the sleeve. Trim and press the seam towards the cuff.

21 On the outside of the sleeve, pin the pressed edge of the cuff facing over the seam. Stitch close to the pressed edge.

22 Roll the cuff to the outside of the sleeve. Anchor the cuff to the back sleeve seam with a few hand stitches between the top shaping.

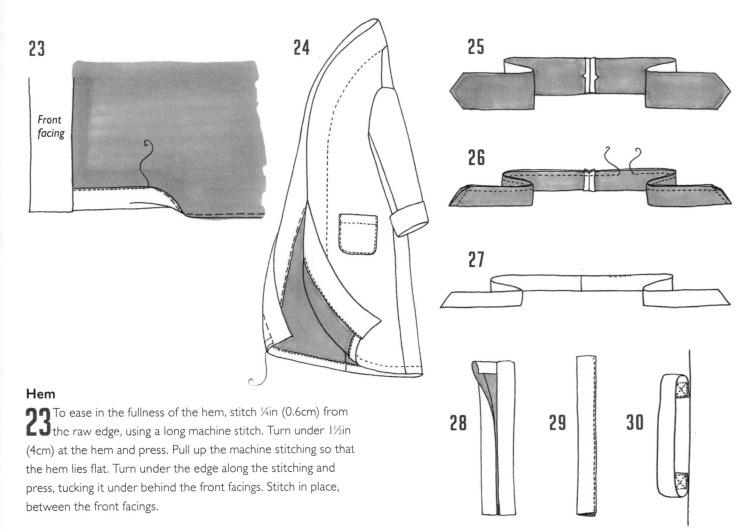

Hem

23 To ease in the fullness of the hem, stitch ¼in (0.6cm) from the raw edge, using a long machine stitch. Turn under 1½in (4cm) at the hem and press. Pull up the machine stitching so that the hem lies flat. Turn under the edge along the stitching and press, tucking it under behind the front facings. Stitch in place, between the front facings.

24 Tack the sides of the facing down, close to the pressed edges. Topstitch along the tacking line and then remove the tacking stitches.

Belt

25 With right sides together, pin and stitch the two belt pieces together across the straight ends to make one long length. Press the seam open.

26 With right sides together, fold the belt along the line indicated on the pattern. Stitch all around, leaving an opening to turn. Trim the seams and cut diagonally across the corners, taking care not to cut into the stitching.

27 Turn the belt right side out and press. Slipstitch (see page 154) the opening closed.

Belt loops

28 To make the loops to carry the belt, cut two 4¾ x 1½in (12 x 4cm) pieces of fabric. Turn under ¼in (0.6cm) at each short end, turn the long edges in to the centre and press.

29 Fold the strip in half lengthways and stitch along the long, unfolded edge, close to the pressed edges.

30 Sew the short ends of each loop in place at the dots on the side seams of the back of the garment. Thread the belt through the loops.

SLIPPERS

These low-back slippers are ideal for the gentleman who likes to travel, as they are light to carry and take up very little luggage space. The insole and upper part of each slipper are cut in one piece with a separate sole.

FABRIC REQUIRED

40 x 19¾in (100 x 50cm) of ⅛–¼in (0.3–0.6cm) thick wool felt

PATTERN PIECES

From pattern sheet F:

68 Sole (cut 2)
69 Upper and insole (cut 2)

SEWING NOTIONS

Thread to match the fabric
Sewing needle

SEAM ALLOWANCES

Take ¼in (0.6cm) seam allowances throughout, unless otherwise stated

FINISHED MEASUREMENTS

See page 147 for shoe sizes and how to measure your feet

Slippers cutting layout

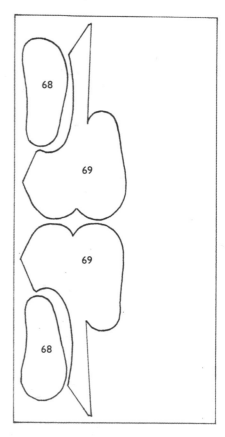

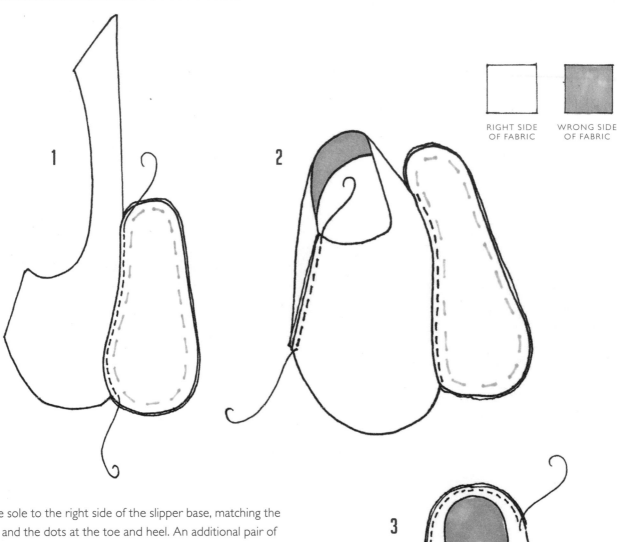

RIGHT SIDE
OF FABRIC

WRONG SIDE
OF FABRIC

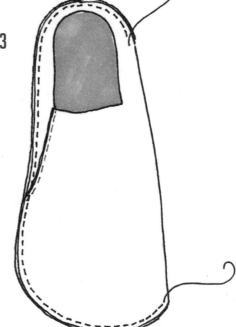

1 Tack the sole to the right side of the slipper base, matching the shaping and the dots at the toe and heel. An additional pair of soles can be cut from leather to make the slippers more durable. Attach these along with the felt sole. Using the thread doubled, sew the inner edge of the sole to the slipper with a double running stitch (see page 155).

2 With wrong sides together, join the diagonal seam of the upper with a double running stitch.

3 With wrong sides together, pin and stitch the outer edges together with a double running stitch as before, matching the medium dots at the toe, the large dots at the heel and the seam on the side of the upper to the small dot. Sew through all layers of the upper, insole and sole of the slipper. Remove the tacking stitches. Repeat steps 1–3 to finish the other slipper, making sure the pieces are flipped to form a matching pair.

Accoutrements

PATTERN PIECES

From pattern sheets D and E:

70 Strap (cut 2 in main fabric)

71 Flap (cut 1 in main fabric, cut 1 in lining fabric, cut 1 in interfacing)

72 Base (cut 1 in main fabric, cut 1 in lining fabric, cut 1 in interfacing, cut 1 in buckram)

73 Front and back (cut 2 in main fabric, cut 2 in lining fabric, cut 2 in interfacing)

74 Front pocket (cut 2 in main fabric; cut 2 in lining fabric for inside pocket)

75 Side, bottom (cut 2 in main fabric, cut 2 in interfacing, cut 2 in buckram)

76 Tab (cut 2 in main fabric)

77 Side, top (cut 2 in main fabric, cut 2 in interfacing, cut 2 in buckram)

78 Side lining (cut 2 in lining fabric)

79 Small long pocket (cut 2 in lining fabric)

80 Small wide pocket (cut 2 in lining fabric)

MESSENGER BAG

This roomy bag is lined and features an adjustable shoulder strap and a flap opening with magnetic clasps to fasten. It has a large front pocket as well as inside pockets, and pouches to hold smaller items.

FABRIC REQUIRED

Refer to the appropriate column for your fabric width.

FABRIC WIDTH (WITHOUT NAP)	MAIN FABRIC	LINING FABRIC
36in (90cm)	2yd (1.8m)	1⅝yd (1.5m)
45in (115cm)	1¾yd (1.6m)	1¼yd (1.1m)
60in (150cm)	1¾yd (1.6m)	1¼yd (1.1m)
36in (90cm) medium- to heavy-weight sew-in interfacing	1¼yd (1.1m)	1¼yd (1.1m)

SUGGESTED FABRICS

For main fabric: Waxed cotton/oilskin, denim, corduroy, canvas, tweed
For lining: Cotton, glazed cotton, canvas, duck canvas

SEWING NOTIONS

Thread to match the fabric
⅓yd (0.3m) of 23½in (60cm) wide buckram
2in (5cm) three-bar slider
2 x 2in (5cm) two-bar sliders
2 x ¾in (2cm) magnetic sew-on clasps

SEAM ALLOWANCES

Take ⅝in (1.5cm) seam allowances throughout, unless otherwise stated

FINISHED MEASUREMENTS

15 x 11¾ x 3½in (38 x 30 x 9cm)

PATTERN NOTE

If using waxed cotton/oilskin, do not use an iron, but run the closed blades of your fabric scissors along the seams to press them open. When pinning and tacking waxed cotton/oilskin, work close to the raw edges, so any holes are within the seam line and won't show. When choosing the main fabric and lining, remember layers of heavier fabric can be tricky to work with, especially when topstitching. Before topstitching, test on scraps of fabric. Work slowly and carefully on the machine and turn the wheel by hand if necessary, especially at the corners, where the seams are bulkier. Use the correct size needle for the fabric weight (see page 139).

Main fabric – 36, 45, 60in (90, 115, 150cm) wide

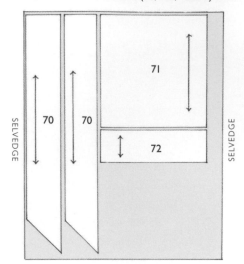

Main fabric – 36in (90cm) wide

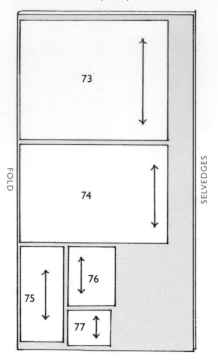

Main fabric – 45, 60in (115, 150cm) wide

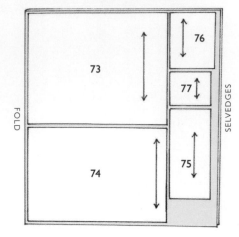

Interfacing – 36in (90cm) wide

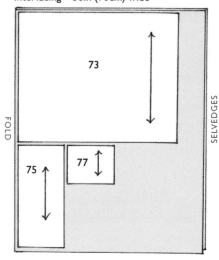

Lining fabric – 36in (90cm) wide

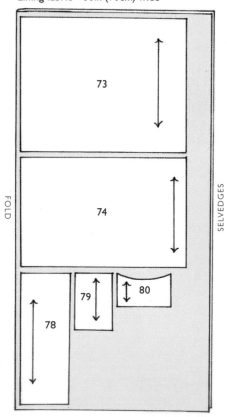

Lining fabric – 45 & 60in (115 & 150cm) wide

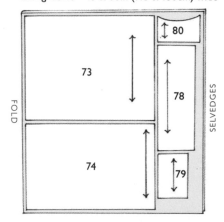

Lining fabric – 36, 45, 60in (90, 115, 150cm) wide
& interfacing 36in (90cm) wide

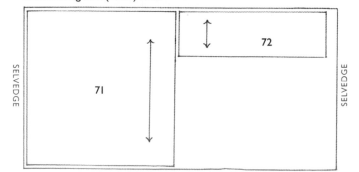

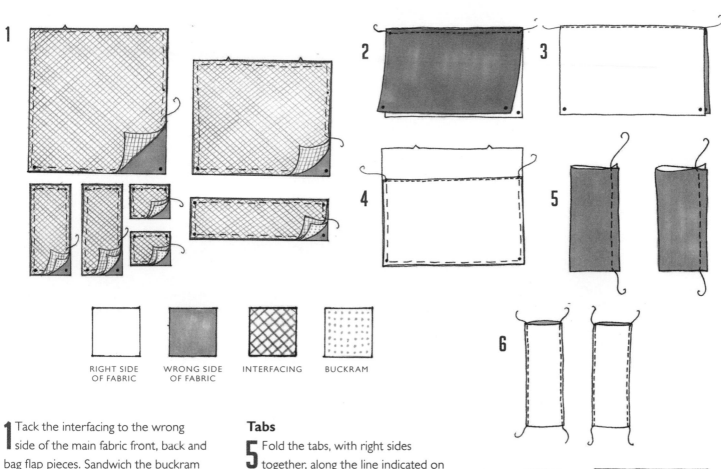

RIGHT SIDE
OF FABRIC

WRONG SIDE
OF FABRIC

INTERFACING

BUCKRAM

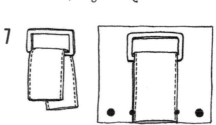

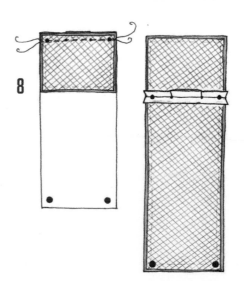

1 Tack the interfacing to the wrong side of the main fabric front, back and bag flap pieces. Sandwich the buckram between the interfacing and the wrong side of the matching main fabric side and base pieces. Tack in place.

Front pocket

2 With right sides together, pin and stitch the top edges of the front pocket pieces together.

3 Turn right side out and press (using the closed blades of the fabric scissors if working with oilskin). Topstitch close to the stitched edge.

4 Place the pocket on the right side of the front main fabric piece, matching the dots. Tack them together along the side and lower edges to hold the layers in place.

Tabs

5 Fold the tabs, with right sides together, along the line indicated on the pattern and stitch the long edge.

6 Turn right side out and press. Topstitch down each long side, close to the edges.

7 Slip the end of the tab through the two-bar slider. With the short ends together to form a loop, place the tab on the right side of the top side piece, matching the small dots. Tack in place.

8 With right sides together, stitch the top and bottom side pieces together, matching the medium dots. Work a second row of stitching over the first to reinforce the seam. Press the seam open.

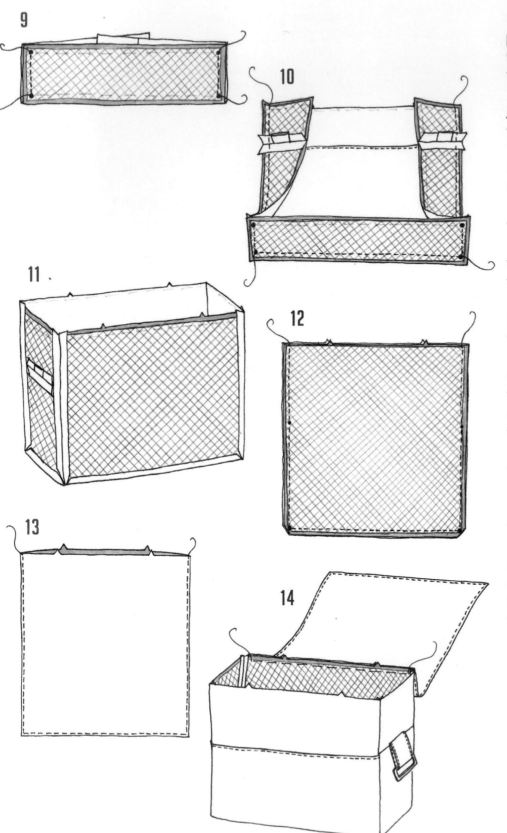

Sides and base

9 With right sides together, pin and stitch the sides to the base between the large dots.

Join front and back

10 With right sides together, pin and stitch the front of the bag to the sides and base between the large dots, sewing through all layers.

11 Join the back of the bag to the sides and base in the same way. Cut across the corners, taking care not to cut into the stitching. Press the seams open.

Bag flap

12 With right sides together, matching the dots and notches, stitch the main fabric bag flap to the lining, leaving the notched end open. Layer the seams and cut diagonally across the corners, taking care not to cut the stitching.

13 Turn the flap right side out and press. Topstitch close to the stitched edges.

14 Turn the bag right side out and carefully poke out the corners with a knitting needle or a pin. With the front of the flap against the right side of the back of the bag, matching the notches, tack the flap to the bag.

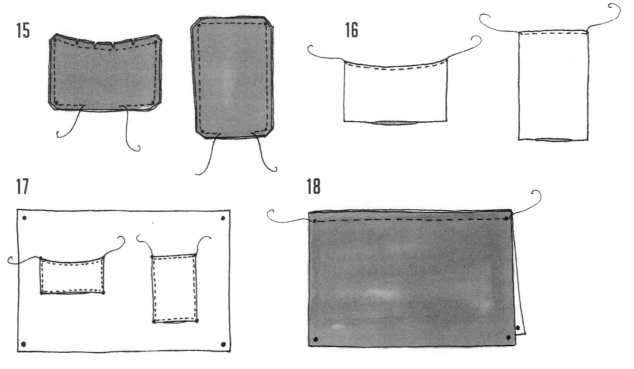

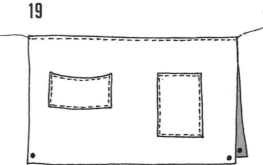

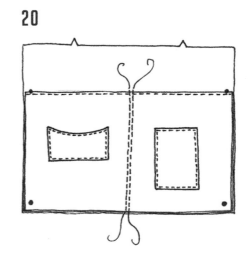

Inside pockets

15 With right sides together and matching the dots and shaping, pin and stitch the edges of the two sets of small pocket pieces, allowing ⅜in (1cm) seam and leaving a gap in the lower edges to turn. Trim the seams, snip the curve (see page 158) and cut diagonally across the corners, taking care not to cut into the stitching.

16 Turn right side out and press. Topstitch (see page 156) along the top edges of the pockets.

17 Place both of the small pockets on the right side of one inside pocket piece, matching the small dots. Stitch close to the side and lower edges, closing the openings that were left in the lower edges of the pockets at the same time.

Take particular care if using a heavier lining fabric such as canvas. Work slowly and turn the wheel of the machine by hand if necessary, especially at the corners where the seams will be bulkier.

18 With right sides together, matching the dots, pin and stitch the top edges of the inside pocket pieces together, along the ⅝in (1.5cm) seam line.

19 Turn right side out and press. Topstitch along the top edge.

20 Place the inside pocket, facing up, on top of the right side of the back lining piece, matching the dots. Work a double row of stitches down the centre of the pocket, as indicated by the broken lines on the pattern, sewing through all layers.

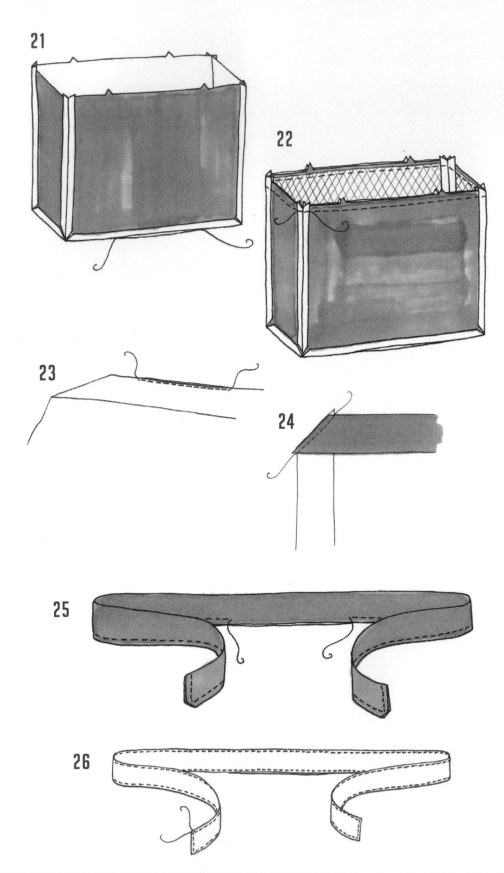

Join lining pieces

21 Follow steps 9–11 of the main fabric bag to join the front and back to the sides and base, leaving a gap of around 8in (20cm) along one lower edge.

Join lining to bag

22 With right sides together, slip the main bag inside the lining, sandwiching the flap between them and matching the seams and notches. The lining pockets should be at the back of the bag. Stitch the main bag and lining together around the top edges.

23 Pull the bag, through the opening in the lining, to the right side. To close the opening in the bag lining, with wrong sides together, pin and stitch close to the edges.

Strap

24 Join the two lengths of fabric by stitching the diagonal ends together, with the wrong sides together and the pieces at right angles to each other. Press the seam flat.

25 With right sides together, fold the strap along the line indicated on the pattern. Pin and stitch the edges, leaving a gap of around 15¾in (40cm) in the long edge to turn. Cut diagonally across the corners, taking care not to cut into the stitching.

26 Turn the strap right side out and press. Turn under and press the seam allowance at the opening. Topstitch the strap, close to the edges.

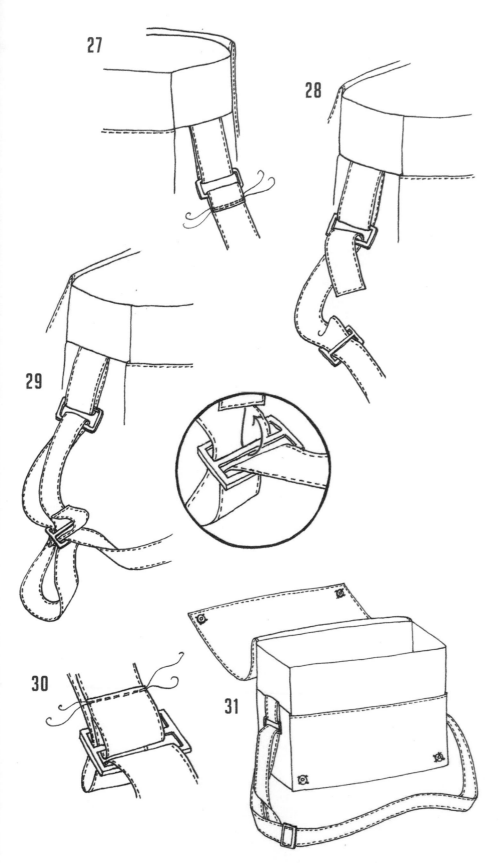

27 With the front of the bag facing, insert one end of the strap up through the slider attached to the tab on the right-hand side. Sew the end of the strap down, working two lines of stitches close to each other to reinforce the join.

28 Insert the other end of the strap up through the first opening of the three-bar slider, over the central bar and then back down through the second opening. Next, insert the same end up through the slider attached to the left-hand tab.

29 Pull the strap away from the central bar of the slider to make it easier to thread the end through again. Insert the end back through the first opening, over the bar and through the second opening.

30 Adjust the strap to loosen it around the three-bar slider and stitch the end in place, working two lines of stitches close to each other to reinforce the join.

Fastening

31 Sew the magnetic clasps (see page 171) to the front pocket and the lining of the flap, indicated by a + on the pattern pieces, to fasten the messenger bag.

WALLET

PATTERN PIECES

From pattern sheet F:

81 Bank note pocket (cut 2 in lining fabric)
82 Pocket (cut 3 in lining fabric)
83 Coin pouch flap (cut 2 in lining fabric, cut 1 in interfacing)
84 Coin pouch (cut 2 in lining fabric)
85 Card holder (cut 1 in lining fabric)
86 Cover (cut 1 in main fabric, cut 1 in lining fabric, cut 1 in interfacing)
87 Tab (cut 1 in main fabric, cut 1 in lining fabric, cut 1 in interfacing)

The wallet has a large pocket for bank notes, a tiered section to hold bank cards, a coin pouch and two small pockets. A second card holder can replace the coin pouch if it is not required.

FABRIC REQUIRED

⅓ x ⅓yd (0.3 x 0.3m) of main fabric

½yd (0.45m) of 36, 45, 60in (90, 115, 150cm) wide fabric for the lining and the inner sections

¼yd (0.2m) of 36in (90cm) wide light-weight interfacing

⅓ x ⅓yd (0.3 x 0.3m) of fabric for the binding

SUGGESTED FABRICS

For cover: Tweed, denim, canvas, boiled wool
For lining and inner sections: Light- to medium-weight fabrics, such as quilting cotton, cotton shirting, glazed cotton, chambray

SEWING NOTIONS

Thread to match the fabric
2 x ⅜in (1cm) snap fastenings

SEAM ALLOWANCES

Take ⅜in (1cm) seam allowances throughout, unless otherwise stated

FINISHED MEASUREMENTS

4¾ x 4¾in (12 x 12cm)

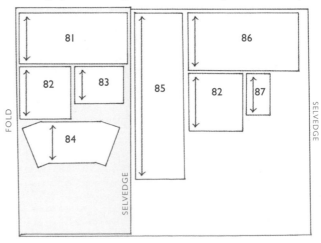

Cutting layout for lining and inner sections (all fabric widths)

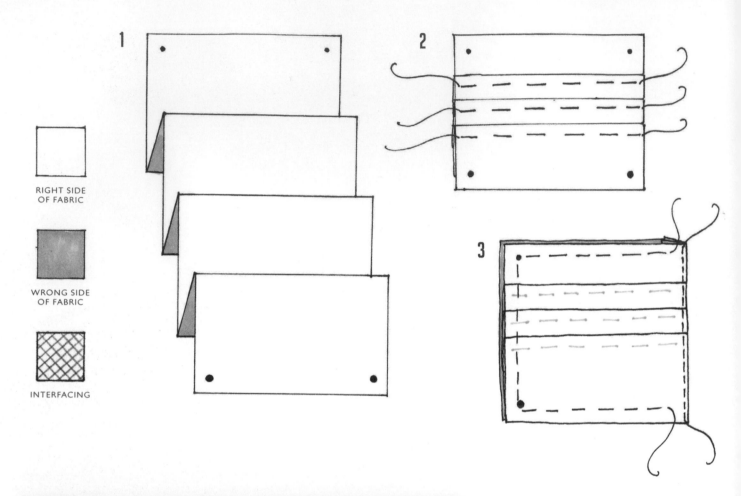

RIGHT SIDE
OF FABRIC

WRONG SIDE
OF FABRIC

INTERFACING

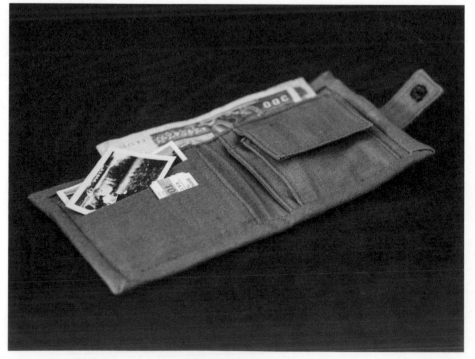

Card holder

1 Press along the fold lines of the card holder to form pockets.

2 Tack along the pressed edges to hold them in place.

3 With right sides together, sew the right-hand side edges of the card holder and one pocket lining piece together, stitching through all layers. This will be on the inside edge of the wallet, forming a small pocket. Layer the seam to reduce bulk (see Clipping Seams, page 158). Turn right side out and press. Topstitch close to the stitched edge. Tack the top, outside and lower edges to hold the layers of fabric in place.

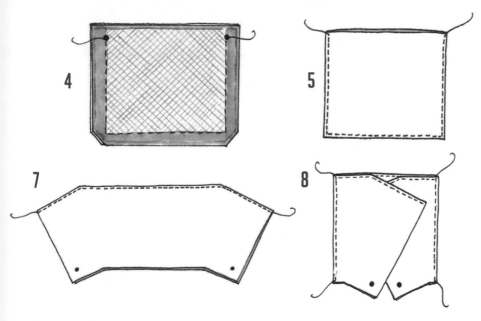

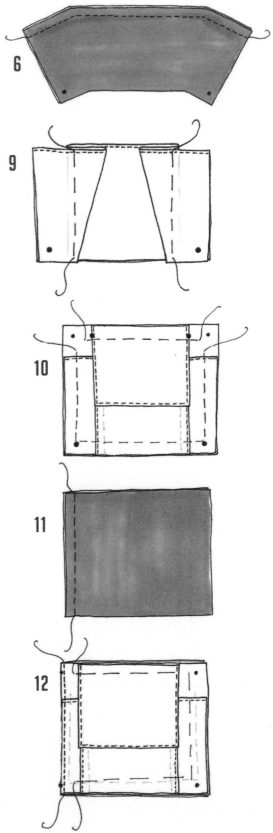

Coin pouch

4 Following the manufacturer's instructions, apply iron-on interfacing to the wrong side of one of the coin pouch flap pieces. With right sides together, stitch the flap pieces together, leaving the top edge open to turn. Trim the seams and cut diagonally across the corners, taking care not to cut into the stitches.

5 Turn right side out and press. Topstitch close to the stitched edges.

6 With right sides together, stitch the top edges of the coin pouch together.

7 Trim the seam, turn right side out and press. Topstitch close to the top edge.

8 Turn under and press along the inner fold lines, indicated on the pattern. Topstitch close to the pressed edges.

9 Fold back the outer lines, indicated on the pattern, and press. Tack each side to hold them in place.

10 Place the coin pouch, front facing up, on top of the right side of one pocket lining piece, matching the dots and aligning the raw edges. Tack the side and lower edges together. Place the flap, with the interfaced piece underneath, on top of the right side of the same pocket lining piece, matching the dots and overlapping the top of the coin pouch. Tack along the top edge of the flap.

11 Place the right side of the remaining pocket lining piece on top, sandwiching the coin pouch and flap between the two layers of lining. Sew the left-hand side edges together, stitching through all layers. This will be on the inside edge of the wallet, forming a small pocket. Layer the seam.

12 Turn right side out and press. Topstitch close to the stitched inside edge. Tack the outside, top and lower edges to hold the layers in place.

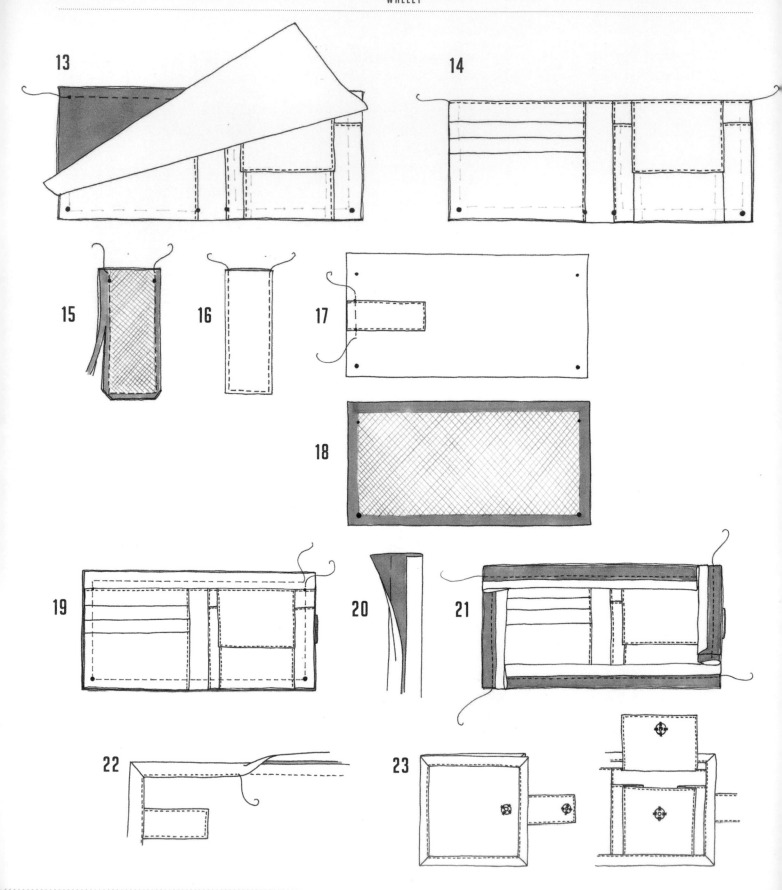

13

14

15

16

17

18

19

20

21

22

23

Bank note pocket

13 With right sides facing up, lay the card holder and coin pouch on top of the right side of one of the bank note pocket pieces, matching the dots and aligning the raw edges. The stitched inside edges of the card holder and coin pouch should face towards the centre. Place the remaining bank note piece with right side facing down on top, enclosing the card holder and coin pouch. Sew the top edges together, stitching through all layers. Layer the seam to reduce bulk.

14 Turn right side out and press. Topstitch (see page 156) along the top edge.

Tab fastening

15 Following the manufacturer's instructions, apply iron-on interfacing to the wrong side of the tab lining. With right sides together, sew the tab pieces together, leaving one short end open to turn. Trim the seams and cut diagonally across the corners, taking care not to cut into the stitching.

16 Turn right side out and press. Topstitch close to the stitched edges of the tab.

17 Position the tab onto the right side of the cover with the lining facing up, aligning the raw edges and matching the dots. Tack in place.

18 Following the manufacturer's instructions, apply iron-on interfacing to the wrong side of the wallet cover lining.

19 With wrong sides together and the tab on the right-hand side, place the wallet cover lining on top of the wallet cover. Place the bank note pocket, with the attached card holder and coin pouch facing up, on the right side of the wallet cover lining fabric, aligning the lower and side edges and matching the dots. Pin and stitch around the edges, sewing through all layers. Remove the tacking stitches.

Binding

20 Cut 1½in (4cm) wide bias strips from the fabric and sew the short edges together to make 1yd (0.9m) of binding (see page 166). Press ⅜in (1cm) seam allowance along each long edge.

21 Open out one pressed edge of the binding. Turn under ⅜in (1cm) at the short end. With the right side of the binding to the inside of the wallet, pin and stitch the creased edge of the binding to the ⅜in (1cm) seam allowance of the wallet, overlapping the end and folding out the fullness of the binding at the corners (see page 167). Press the seams towards the binding.

22 Turn the binding to the right side of the wallet to encase the seam allowances. Pin the pressed edge over the seams. Topstitch (see page 156) close to the pressed edges, or slipstitch (see page 154) the binding in place. Slipstitch the mitred corners. Press the bound edges.

23 Sew a snap fastening (see page 171) to fasten the tab closure and the pocket flap of the coin compartment, indicated by a + on the pattern pieces.

BOW TIE

This can be made in self-tie or ready-tied styles. The ready-tied version has a hook-and-eye fastening, while a slider, threaded through the band of the bow tie, allows the wearer to adjust both styles to fit.

FABRIC REQUIRED

Refer to the appropriate column for your clothing size and the fabric width.

36in (90cm)	⅞yd (0.80m)
45in (115cm)	⅞yd (0.80m)
60in (150cm)	⅞yd (0.80m)
36in (90cm) underlining (optional)	⅞ yd (0.80m)

PATTERN PIECES

From pattern sheet F:

88 Bow tie (cut 2 long and 2 short in main fabric, cut 2 long and 2 short in underlining, if using)

SUGGESTED FABRICS

Satin, silk, cotton, velvet

SEWING NOTIONS

Thread to match the fabric
¾in (2cm) bow tie slider
¾in (2cm) hook-and-eye fastening for the ready-tied version, or the eye only for the self-tie version

SEAM ALLOWANCES

Take ⅝in (1.5cm) seam allowances throughout, unless otherwise stated

FINISHED MEASUREMENTS

2¼in (5.75cm) at widest part
Adjustable length

36, 45 and 60in (90, 115 and 150cm) wide fabric

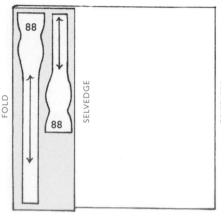

1 If underlining (see page 145) is being added to the bow tie, prepare the cut fabric before sewing by tacking the underlining to the wrong side of the matching main pieces. With right sides together, matching the shaping, pin and stitch the short pieces of the bow tie pieces together, leaving the wide end open to turn. Join the long pieces in the same way. Trim the seams and cut diagonally into the corners, taking care not to cut the stitching.

2 Turn the two sections of the bow tie right side out and press. Turn under the seam allowance and slipstitch (see page 154) the opening at the wide end of each piece to close.

3 Slip the narrow end of the long piece of the bow tie through the slider, inserting up through the first opening, over the bar in the centre of the slider and then back down through the second opening. Next, slip the same end through the eye part of the fastening, making sure the loop of the eye is facing upwards.

4 Lift the band of the bow tie away from the central bar of the slider to make it easier to thread the end through again. Insert the end back through the first opening, over the bar and through the second opening.

5 Stitch the end to the back of the band neatly by hand.

Ready-tied version

6 Thread the narrow end of the short piece of the bow tie through the hook and neatly hand sew the end to the back of the band. Fasten the hook and eye.

7 To tie the bow tie, put it around your neck so one end is longer than the other (a). Cross the long end over the short end (b), pass the long end under and back over the neck loop. Fold the short end to form the bow shape and hold it in position (c).

8 Bring the long end over the front of the centre of the bow shape (d). Fold the long end to form a second bow shape (e) and push the folded end through the loop behind the first bow shape. Pull the folded ends to tighten the bow (f).

9 Work a few stitches at the back, through the edges of the knot and into the band and back of the bow to keep it from coming undone.

Self-tied version

10 Thread the narrow end of the short piece of the bow tie through the same eye as the long end is attached to. Neatly hand sew the end to the back of the band, ensuring both ends are stitched at the back of the bow tie. Follow steps 7-8 to tie the bow tie.

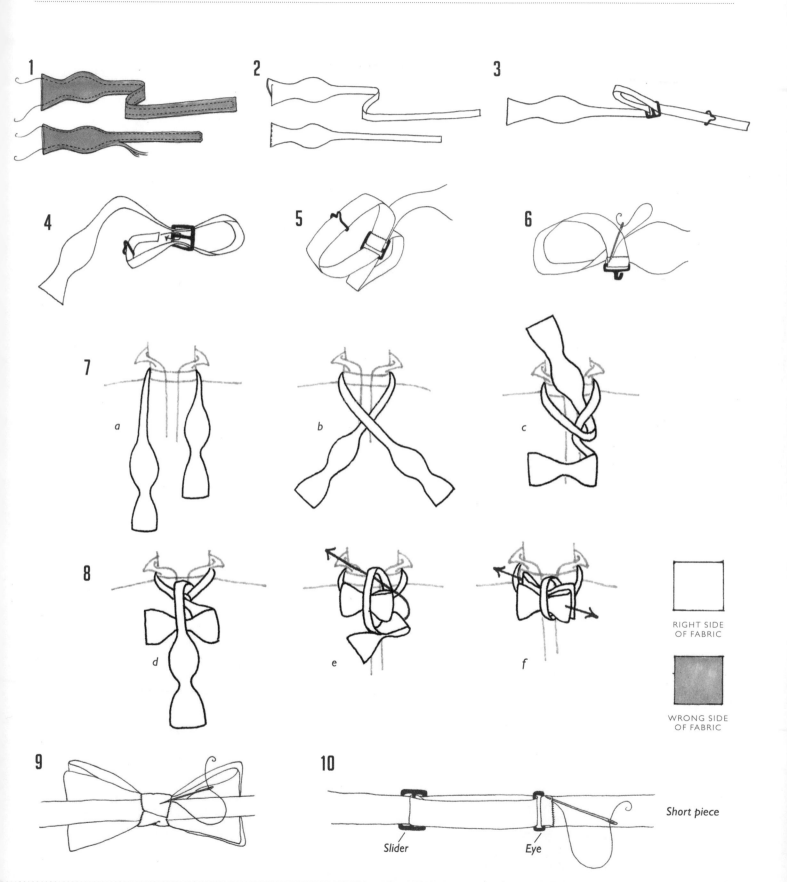

1

2

3

4

5

6

7

a

b

c

8

d

e

f

RIGHT SIDE
OF FABRIC

WRONG SIDE
OF FABRIC

9

10

Short piece

Slider

Eye

CRAVAT

Choose a soft fabric with drape for this elegant project. The cravat is simple to make with just one piece to cut out and very little sewing involved. Pleats form the detail at the back of the neck.

FABRIC REQUIRED

Refer to the appropriate column for your clothing size and the fabric width.

36in (90cm)	1⅜yd (1.3m)
45in (115cm)	1⅜yd (1.3m)
60in (90cm)	1⅜yd (1.3m)

PATTERN PIECES

From pattern sheet A:

89 Cravat (cut 1)

SUGGESTED FABRICS

Fabrics with drape, such as silk, satin, crepe, light-weight wool

SEWING NOTIONS

Thread to match fabric

SEAM ALLOWANCES

Take ⅝in (1.5cm) seam allowances throughout, unless otherwise stated

FINISHED MEASUREMENTS

5¼ × 44½in (13.5 × 113cm) at widest and longest parts

36, 45 and 60in (90, 115 and 150cm) wide fabric

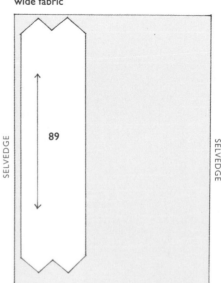

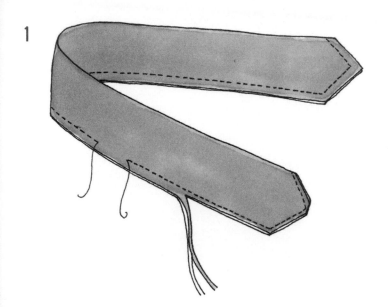

1

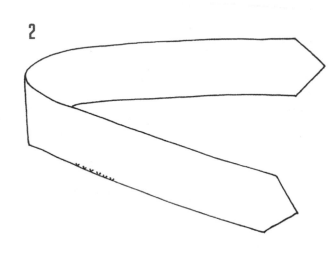

2

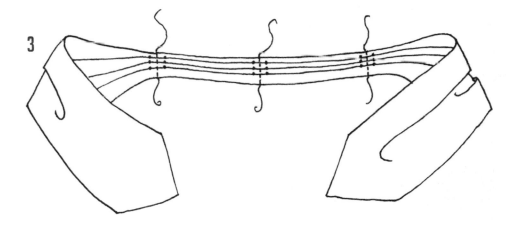

3

1 With right sides together, fold the cravat along the line indicated on the pattern. Stitch around the edges, leaving an opening on the long edge to turn. Trim the seams and cut straight across the pointed ends, taking care not to cut the stitching.

2 Turn the cravat right side out and press. Slipstitch (see page 154) the opening closed.

3 To make the pleats, bring the short lines together, following the direction of the arrows and matching the small dots to the large dots above them. Tack and stitch along the broken lines indicated on the pattern. Remove the tacking stitches.

RIGHT SIDE
OF FABRIC

WRONG SIDE
OF FABRIC

FLAT CAP

PATTERN PIECES

From pattern sheet F:

90 Top (cut 1 in main fabric, cut 1 in lining fabric, cut 1 in hair canvas)

91 Side (cut 1 in main fabric, cut 1 in lining fabric, cut 1 in hair canvas)

92 Peak (cut 2 in main fabric, cut 2 in hair canvas)

93 Peak template (cut 1 in buckram)

Make this cap in a tweed fabric for a traditional look, or use denim for a contemporary twist. The deep peak is ideal for shading the eyes from the sun or providing some protection from the elements on a rainy day.

FABRIC REQUIRED

Refer to the appropriate column for your hat size.

ALL FABRIC WIDTHS (WITHOUT NAP)	SMALL	MEDIUM	LARGE
Main fabric:	½yd (0.45m)	½yd (0.45m)	½yd (0.45m)
Lining fabric:	½yd (0.45m)	½yd (0.45m)	½yd (0.45m)
23½in (60cm) sew-in hair canvas	1yd (0.9m)	1yd (0.9m)	1yd (0.9m)

SUGGESTED FABRICS

For main fabric: Tweed, wool, denim, corduroy, canvas

For lining: Cotton shirting, cotton, cotton mix

SEWING NOTIONS

Thread to match the fabric

9 x 9in (23 x 23cm) of heavy buckram

1yd (0.9m) of 1in (2.5cm) wide petersham ribbon

SEAM ALLOWANCES

Take ⅜in (1cm) seam allowances throughout, unless otherwise stated

FINISHED MEASUREMENTS

See page 146 for hat sizes and how to measure your head

Main fabric (all widths), lining fabric and interfacing

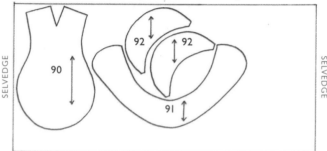

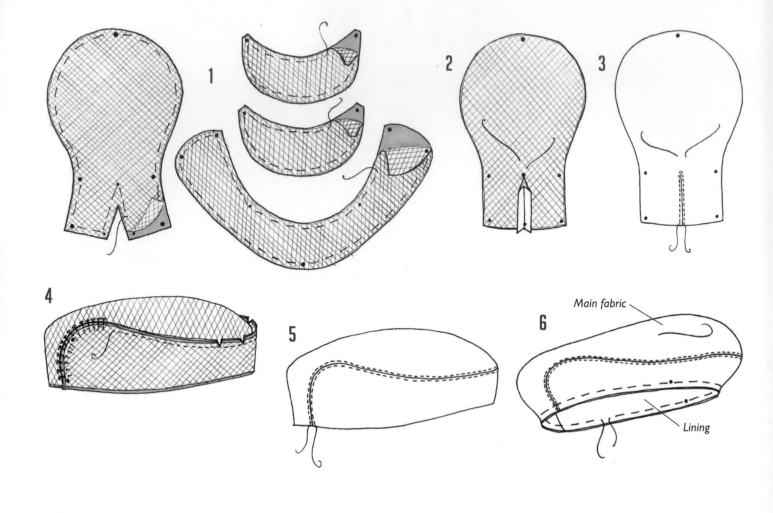

Main fabric

Lining

RIGHT SIDE OF FABRIC

WRONG SIDE OF FABRIC

HAIR CANVAS

BUCKRAM

1 Tack the hair canvas to the wrong side of the main fabric top, side and peak pieces.

2 Stitch the dart at the centre back of the top of the cap (see page 161). Slash to within ½in (1.25cm) of the point of the dart and press open.

3 Topstitch (see page 156) along each side of the dart seam.

4 With right sides together, matching the dots, pin the side to the top piece. Insert plenty of pins to ease the fabric

of the top of the cap around the curves of the sides. Stitch together. Notch the curves (see page 158) and press the seams towards the top of the cap.

5 Topstitch (see page 156) along each side of the seams.

Lining

6 Follow steps 2 and 4, omitting the topstitching, to join the top and side lining pieces. With wrong sides together, matching the dots and seams, pin the main piece to the lining. Tack the lower edges together.

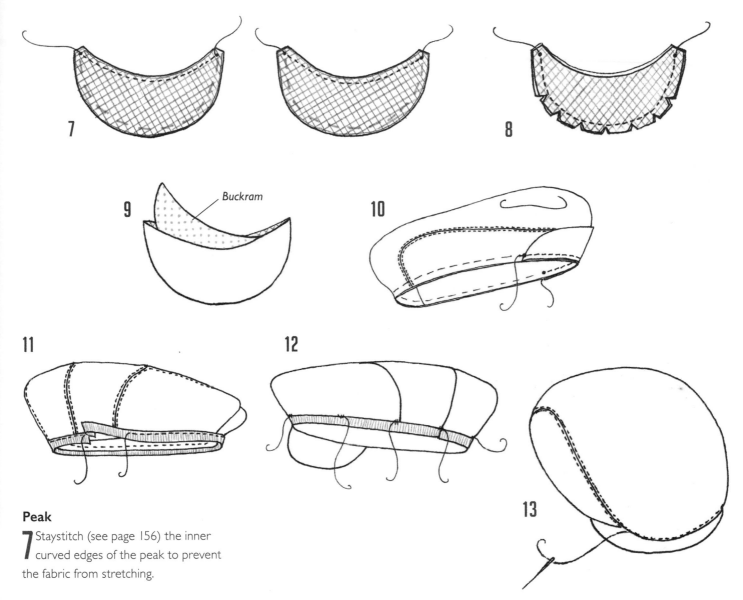

Buckram

Peak

7 Staystitch (see page 156) the inner curved edges of the peak to prevent the fabric from stretching.

8 With right sides together, stitch the peak pieces together, leaving the inner curved edge open to turn. Trim and notch the seam.

9 Turn right side out and press. Insert the buckram and tack the open edges of the peak together.

10 Stitch the peak to the side piece of the cap, matching the dots. Notch the seam.

Ribbon

11 Placing one end of the ribbon just over the centre back dart seam, pin the edge of the ribbon around the seam line on the outside of the lower edge of the cap. Turn under the other end of the ribbon and align it with the dart seam at the centre back. Stitch the ribbon to the cap along the seam line.

12 Turn the ribbon to the inside of the cap and press. Catch the ribbon to the lining in a number of places with a few stitches.

13 Press the cap. Hand stitch the peak to the front of the side piece of the cap.

Techniques

SEWING TOOLS

For the beginner, just a few basic items are essential for successful sewing. As your skills increase, more complicated equipment can be added to your toolbox.

MEASURING AND MARKING EQUIPMENT

Tape measure

A tape measure is a vital piece of equipment for dressmaking. A PVC tape is preferable, as it won't stretch or tear like a fabric or paper one.

Sewing gauge

The gauge has a sliding pointer that can be set to the length required for measuring hems and seam allowances precisely, and also for the marking of tucks and pleats.

Tailor's chalk

Tailor's chalk is used for marking pattern shapes on fabric and can be brushed away. It comes in white for use on dark cloth and in various colours for use on light fabric. It should be kept sharp for a clean line. The chalk can also be found in the form of a pencil.

Tracing wheel

A tracing wheel is mainly used for marking and duplicating lines on paper patterns and transferring pattern lines to fabric. It has a finely spiked wheel with very sharp points that will not tear the paper. The wheels should not be used on silks because the spikes can tear the fine threads of the fabric.

Carbon paper

Dressmaker's carbon paper is used in the same way as the traditional stationery kind for copying documents. This type is heavier, making it easy to pin to fabric without tearing. It is available in yellow, white, blue and red, to work with light and dark fabrics.

CUTTING EQUIPMENT

Shears

Tailor's and dressmaking shears have long blades and a bent handle so the scissors can rest on the table while cutting, keeping the fabric flat. The blades should be kept sharp for ease of cutting. They must be kept solely for cutting fabric; use a separate pair of scissors for cutting paper patterns.

Small cutting tools

A small pair of very sharp, pointed scissors are ideal for fiddly tasks such as cutting threads close to the work, clipping fabric and unpicking stitches.

Thread clips have one finger ring, designed to hang from the middle finger as you sew. The blades are sprung so they can easily unpick or snip loose threads.

Buttonhole scissors

Buttonhole scissors are useful because they are made specifically for the job, with short, sharp, pointed blades to cut the fabric. They often have an adjustable screw so the buttonhole can be cut to the size required.

Pinking shears

Pinking shears can be used for finishing seams; the jagged blades cut a zigzag line that prevents the fabric from fraying. They should be kept for fabric only, as cutting paper will blunt the blades.

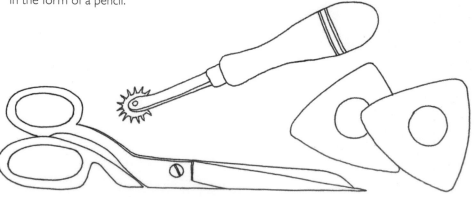

SEWING MACHINE

Many modern sewing machines have a huge variety of stitch selections. However, all the projects in this book can easily be made with a fairly basic machine that does just straight and zigzag stitch. A lot of machines offer automatic buttonholing, which is very useful but not vital. Even an old treadle or hand-operated sewing machine can be used and, if zigzag stitch is not available, the buttonholes can be worked by hand (see page 168).

Care of the machine

Regular maintenance of your sewing machine is essential to keep it running smoothly. Always unplug it before cleaning and oiling.

Lint (a combination of fabric and thread particles) gets caught up near the bobbin and in hidden areas, so should be removed before it causes problems with the machine.

Use proper sewing machine oil and refer to the manual for the areas that need it. Tighten all the screws and then work some machine stitches on scraps of fabric to catch any excess oil.

Using the machine

Have your machine set up in an area with plenty of light and where you can be comfortably seated. Before sewing, make sure that the machine is threaded correctly and that the two threads, from the needle and the bobbin, are placed towards the back of the work. Turn the wheel towards you so that the needle is in the work, preventing a tangle of threads. Every time you begin a new

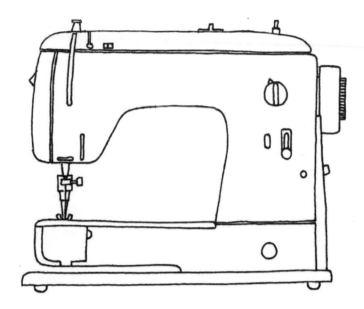

project or use a different type of stitch, practise first on a spare piece of fabric to check the tension and avoid having to unpick mistakes. Taking it slowly will ensure control of the machine and problems with the tension or tangling threads will be less likely to occur.

Machine needles

It is important to use the right size needle for the weight of fabric to produce the best results. Universal needles have a slightly rounded point for use with knitted fabrics but they are sharp enough to go through woven fabrics. For knitted fabrics, a ballpoint needle slips between the fibres of the fabric, preventing snagging. There are also needles specifically for use with denim and leather, and twin needles, used for working two even rows of stitching.

Needle sizes are shown in both imperial and metric. The smallest sizes relate to the finer needles for use with light-weight fabrics. Where the number is larger, the needle is bigger, for sewing medium- to-heavy-weight material.

MACHINE NEEDLE SIZE GUIDE

SIZE	FABRIC EXAMPLES
8/60	Sheer fabrics, chiffon, georgette
10/70	Lining fabrics, cotton lawn
11/80	Shirting fabrics, light-weight cotton
14/90	Cotton sateen, linen
16/100	Denim, canvas
18/110	Leather, vinyl, upholstery fabrics

SMALL NOTIONS

Pins

Pins come in various sizes, for use on fine laces to heavy woven cloth; ones with coloured glass heads are easy to find in fabric. Take care not to use pins that are rusty or blunt – they will damage the fabric.

Thimble

The thimble should fit comfortably, without falling off, protecting the finger that pushes the needle through the fabric.

Beeswax

Beeswax is used for strengthening thread and preventing knots when working buttonholes or inserting zips by hand. It also helps when threading needles. Draw the thread across the beeswax a couple of times to coat it.

Bodkin

A bodkin is used to pull elastic, cord or ribbon through a casing. It looks like a needle with a large eye and blunt end, to prevent it piercing the fabric. Alternatively, a safety pin can be used to feed the item through the casing.

THREADS

When finding thread to match the fabric, choose one that is slightly darker on the reel because it will look lighter when stitched into the fabric. Use a strong thread for sewing seams. Polyester thread is strong and suitable for hand and machine sewing on all fabrics.

Tacking thread is cheaper and, as the stitches are temporary, will break easily. This makes it perfect for the task, but not good for sewing permanent seams. Use a contrast colour for tacking so the stitches are easy to see when they need to be removed.

When sewing on the machine, use the same thread on the bobbin as in the needle. If you are stitching a dark binding to a light fabric, the colour on the bobbin and needle can be changed to match, but don't mix the fibres.

HAND-SEWING NEEDLES

Needles are available in an array of sizes for a multitude of needlework tasks. Make sure they are not rusty and the points are sharp so as not to damage the fabric. The needle should go through the fabric with ease, without leaving a mark or hole.

Sharps

These medium-length needles are used for general sewing and come in various sizes to suit different weights of fabric. They have a relatively large eye to facilitate threading.

Betweens

These are short, slim needles with a round eye, ideal for working small, even stitches.

Straws or milliner's needles

These are long needles used for hat making. They are ideal for tacking or basting.

CLOTH

It is important to have a basic understanding of the fibre content and structure of fabrics, because the characteristics of the cloth will affect the techniques used when working with it, as well as the look of the finished garment.

WOOL

Wool is a softly woven, comfortable and functional fabric. The surface of the fibre is water repellent; the fabric can absorb up to 30% of its weight in moisture without feeling wet, while still retaining its heat.

TWEED

Originally from Scotland, tweed is a durable, textured fabric woven in two or more colours in the Hebrides, Ireland and Yorkshire. The jacket on page 66 was made from a wool and polyamide blend tweed.

SILK

Silk is very luxurious with a strong natural fibre. It is produced from the cocoons spun by the Bombyx mori moth lava (silkworm). Vintage Italian silk was used to make the bow tie and cravat, pages 124 and 128.

LINEN

Linen is made from flax-plant fibres and is a strong fabric that has natural irregularities in the weave. It is cool and comfortable, although it does crease easily. Linen was used for the main fabric of the waistcoat, page 46.

COTTONS

Cotton is very practical and resilient. It can be woven into very fine, sheer fabrics and can also produce durable materials, such as canvas and denim. Cotton shirting was used to make the boxer shorts, page 80.

Waxed cotton/oilskin

This densely woven canvas fabric has been treated with waxes or oils to make the fabric water resistant. When working with this cloth, use tailor's shears to open the seams, rather than pressing with an iron, and pin inside the seam allowance to avoid making holes in the fabric. After time the oil or wax will need to be reapplied. Oilskin was used for the main fabric of the messenger bag, page 110, which was lined in duck canvas (see below).

Duck

Duck is a closely woven, heavy canvas. It is made in various weights and is used for sails, tents and workwear. It is a tough fabric and smooth to the touch.

Glazed cotton

This fabric has had a finishing process that adds sheen to the surface. The treated cloth is rubbed between rollers to polish the fabric. Glazed cotton was used to line the wallet, page 118.

Felted wool

Wool mix

Silk

Linen and
cotton mix

Cotton shirting

Cotton check

Oilskin

Glazed cotton

Tweed

PREPARING FABRIC

Launder washable fabrics before use
so that any shrinkage occurs before the
item is made up. Press the fabric before
you cut out the pattern, making sure the
iron is set to the right heat for the fabric
type. The direction of the grain will affect
the way the finished garment hangs,
so it is very important that the grain of
the fabric is straight before you start a
project. The warp and weft (vertical and
horizontal) threads should be at right
angles to each other.

Straightening the fabric

Straighten the weft edges (the horizontal
threads that lie between the selvedges) by
clipping the fabric at a selvedge edge and
tearing it across, or by withdrawing a few
threads from the fabric and cutting along
the straight line it produces. Straighten
the fabric by stretching on the bias or
crossways until the edges lie together.

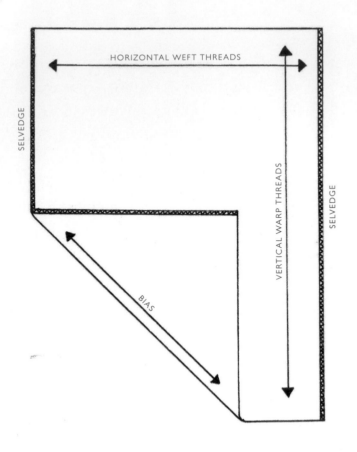

Drawing threads to produce a straight line.

INTERFACING

Interfacing adds structure to an area of a garment, such as a collar or lapel. It is available in light-, medium- or heavyweight versions, to match the weight of the fabric you are using. Interfacing comes in black or charcoal grey for dark fabrics and white for light fabrics.

Woven interfacing has a grain that should be matched with the grain of the fabric that is to be interfaced. Non-woven interfacing can be cut in any direction as it has no grain, making it more economical than woven interfacing. Knitted interfacing is available for use with stretch fabrics. The two main types of interfacing are sew-in and iron-on.

Sew-in interfacing

This is stitched to the fabric and produces a softer drape. It is also used on fabrics that are heat sensitive or open weave and unsuitable for iron-on interfacing.

Iron-on interfacing

Iron-on interfacing has a shiny, fusible side, which is laid on top of the wrong side of the fabric. It is a good idea to test it out on a scrap of material first to check the weight you are using is correct. Make sure that the iron is at the right temperature for the fabric. Place a damp cloth over the pieces and press the iron down for a few seconds, then lift and repeat on another area. Do not drag the iron over the fabric, as it could pucker or move the material. After the interfacing has been fused in place, allow the fabric to cool before stitching.

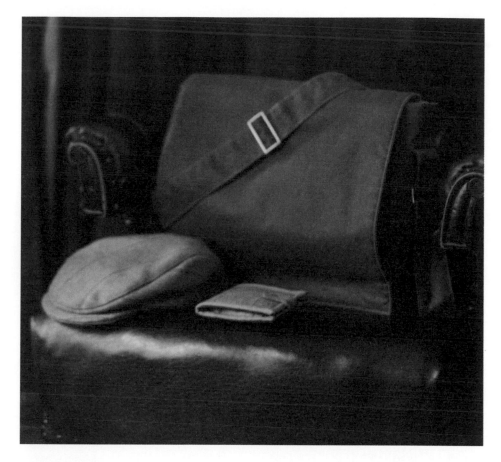

UNDERLINING

Underlining is used to provide body and support to a garment. The main fabric and underlining are cut from the same pattern and handled as one piece. An underlining can be added to the bow tie (see page 124) to help to keep its shape.

HAIR CANVAS

Hair canvas is used in tailoring and is made from horse or goat hair and natural fibres, or a blend of natural and synthetic materials. The hair canvas can be pre-shrunk by spraying it with water and then pressing it with an iron. Hair canvas is used in the flat cap (see page 132).

Buckram is used in the peak of the flat cap, page 132, and for the base of the messenger bag, page 110, to form a really stiff fabric. The wallet, page 118, uses a light-weight iron-on interfacing to give it its structure.

BUCKRAM

Buckram is a stiffened cotton or linen fabric used in millinery. It gives structure to bags and hats, and to curtain pleats and pelmets.

GARMENT SIZES

The patterns in this book have been designed for a comfortable fit, allowing extra for wearing ease. Patterns are in small, medium and large sizes. To help choose the correct size, please refer to the chart.

CLOTHING

GARMENT SIZE	SMALL	MEDIUM	LARGE
Neck	15in (38cm)	15½in (39.5cm)	16in (40.5cm)
Chest	36–38in (90–97cm)	38–40in (97–101cm)	40–42in (101–106cm)
Waist	30–32in (76–81cm)	32–34in (81–86cm)	34–36in (86–90cm)

FOOTWEAR

SLIPPER SIZE	SMALL	MEDIUM	LARGE
UK	6–7	8–9	10–11
US	7–8	9–10	11–12
Continental	40–41	42–43	44–45
Foot length	9⅝–10in (24.5–25.5cm)	10¼–10⅝in (26–27cm)	11–11⅜in (28–29cm)

HATS

HAT SIZE	SMALL	MEDIUM	LARGE
	22in (56cm)	22⅞in (58cm)	23⅝in (60cm)

TAKING MEASUREMENTS

When taking width measurements, such as at the waist, make sure that the tape is parallel to the floor and held taut, but not tight, against the body.

Neck
Measure around the base of the neck. Add ½in (1.25cm) for ease *(1)*.

Chest
With arms at the sides, measure over the largest part of the chest and straight across the back, over the shoulder blades and under arms *(2)*.

Waist
Measure around the natural waistline, midway between bottom of your ribs and the top of your hips *(3)*.

Back waist length
Measure from the neck bone, down the centre back, to the waist *(4)*.

Inside leg
Take this measurement from the top of the inside leg at the crotch to the ankle line *(5)*.

Outside leg
Take this measurement at the side, from the natural waistline to the ankle *(6)*.

Crotch length
Sit on a hard, flat chair and measure from the side of the waist to the seat of the chair. To check your crotch measurement against that of the pattern, measure near the side seam from the widest part of the crotch to the waist. The measurement should match your own with ½–1in (1.25–2.5cm) extra allowed for sitting ease *(7)*.

Hat size
With the tape held close to the head, measure around the circumference of the head, just above the ears *(8)*.

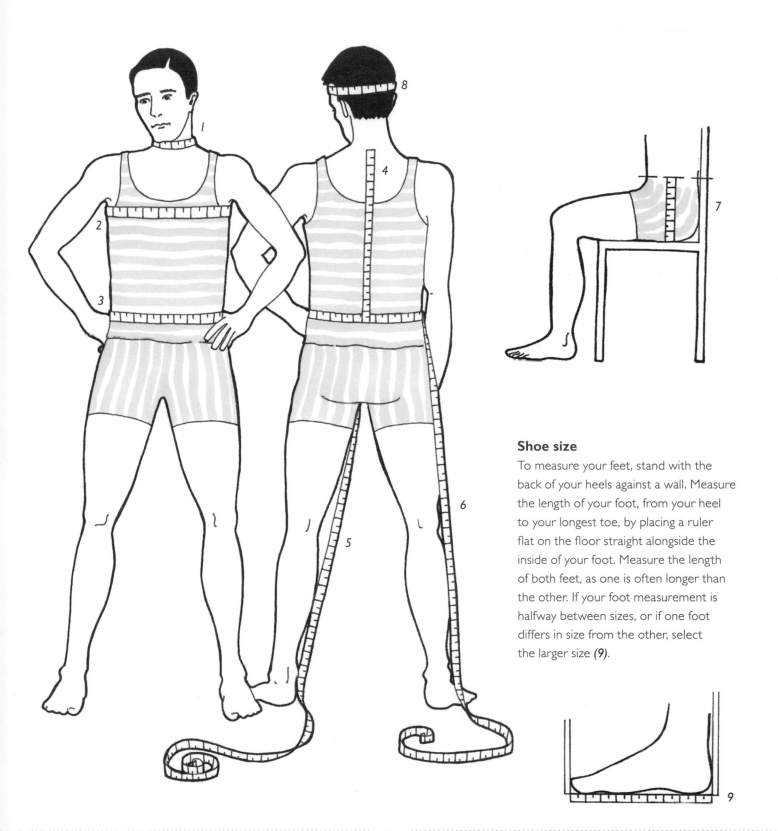

Shoe size

To measure your feet, stand with the back of your heels against a wall. Measure the length of your foot, from your heel to your longest toe, by placing a ruler flat on the floor straight alongside the inside of your foot. Measure the length of both feet, as one is often longer than the other. If your foot measurement is halfway between sizes, or if one foot differs in size from the other, select the larger size *(9)*.

USING THE PATTERN SHEETS

Each pattern piece is numbered so it can be easily identified from the list given at the beginning of each project, as well as making it simple to follow the cutting layouts provided.

FINDING YOUR PATTERN PIECES

Select the pieces needed for the project you are making. These are listed at the beginning of each project and can be found on the pattern sheets at the back of the book. Each sheet has been given a letter for easy reference. The pattern pieces are colour-coded for each project and the individual pieces are numbered. For example, the pattern pieces for the Trousers (see page 54) are found on pattern sheets A, B, D and E, and are numbered 17–26.

COPYING THE PATTERNS

The pattern pieces on the enclosed pattern sheets are printed at actual size, ready to be copied. The patterns can be traced using dressmaker's tissue paper or tracing paper, available in rolls. Another way to copy the patterns is by taking them to a copy shop that can make large copies. They can also be photocopied on a standard photocopier although some of the pieces may need to be taped together if they are larger than your copier paper size. Make sure the patterns are laid flat so they don't distort when copied. Check you have every pattern piece required before you start the project and that you have transferred all the pattern markings (see page 150), ready to use.

CUTTING OUT THE RIGHT SIZE

The garment patterns are in sizes small, medium and large. To calculate the size you need, refer to page 146 for how to take measurements and, based on those measurements, choose the correct size of pattern to cut out. If the gentleman is between sizes, cut out the pattern in the larger size. Each size is labelled along the cutting lines. When tracing or cutting the photocopied pattern pieces, follow the lines according to the size you require.

Patterns can be transferred from a copied pattern sheet using a tracing wheel and carbon paper.

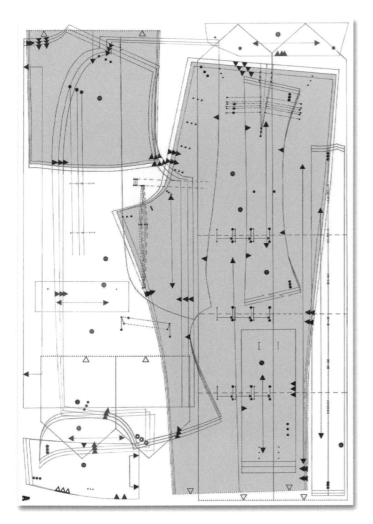

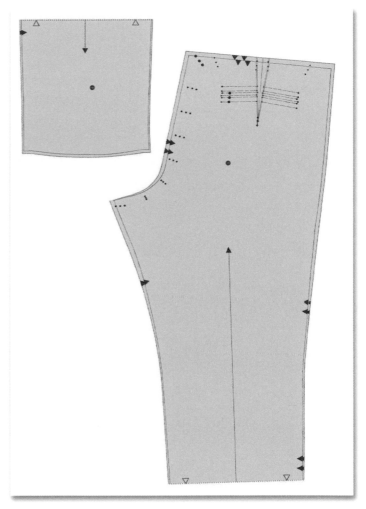

Larger pattern pieces may be split into two parts. These should be joined together by matching up the dotted lines and arrows to make the full pattern piece.

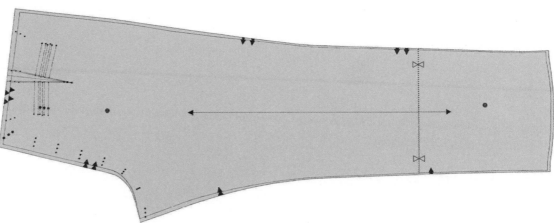

UNDERSTANDING PATTERNS

All the information you need for cutting out and joining seams is given on the pattern pieces. Before you begin to sew, transfer all of the essential markings to your prepared fabric.

Cutting line

The cutting line is a continuous line on the pattern. Seam allowances are given on the pattern pieces as well as in the instructions for each project.

Buttonhole

The positions of the buttonholes are marked on the pattern by solid lines with a bar at each end. The length of the line is the correct length of the buttonhole required for the size of button given in the list of notions at the beginning of each project.

Centre front and centre back

The central line that runs vertically down the front or back is given as CF for the centre front and CB for the centre back.

Sewing lines

A broken line on a pattern, such as along the pocket lines on the jacket, page 66, indicates a sewing line.

Grain lines

When laying out the pattern pieces on the fabric, make sure that the line of the grain, which is marked by a long, double-ended arrow, follows the selvedge of the fabric. Some pattern pieces need to be placed on a fold, which is indicated by the arrows at an angle to the grain line. Fold the fabric so the selvedges are parallel, and place the fold line on the pattern against that of the fabric.

Notches and dots

The notches are used to match the seams accurately when they are sewn together. Where there are two or more notches together on a pattern, cut them in blocks for ease, rather than individually. Match the notches with those of the same number on the piece to be joined. Dots refer to points that should meet on pattern pieces or show where a line of stitching should begin or end.

PATTERN MARKINGS

The markings on a pattern show how it is to be laid on the fabric and cut out, as well as features such as the position of pockets and buttonholes.

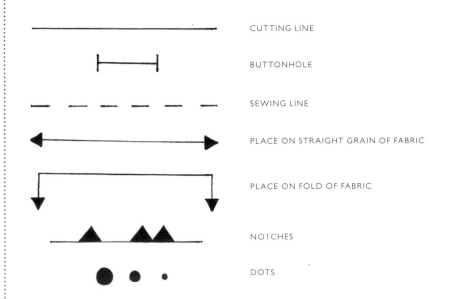

————————	CUTTING LINE
⊢———⊣	BUTTONHOLE
– – – – –	SEWING LINE
◄————►	PLACE ON STRAIGHT GRAIN OF FABRIC
⌐————⌐	PLACE ON FOLD OF FABRIC
▲ ▲▲	NOTCHES
● ● ·	DOTS

ADJUSTING PATTERN LENGTH

Check that all the measurements given for the garment you are making correspond with the gentleman's size. If not, you will need to lengthen or shorten the pattern pieces before cutting out the fabric.

Lengthening pattern pieces

Cut the pattern piece across the width in the areas shown below and place paper behind the pieces. Adjust the pieces so that they are even and are the required distance apart. Stick the pieces to the paper behind with masking tape or sticky tape. Trim the excess paper from each side.

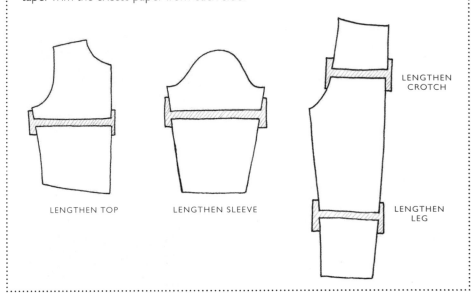

LENGTHEN TOP   LENGTHEN SLEEVE   LENGTHEN LEG

LENGTHEN CROTCH

Shortening pattern pieces

Fold the pattern across the width in the areas shown and overlap the pieces evenly to take up the surplus length required.

SHORTEN TOP   SHORTEN SLEEVE

SHORTEN CROTCH

SHORTEN LEG

HOW TO READ THE 'FABRIC REQUIRED' CHARTS

The length of fabric required can be found on the chart accompanying each project. As fabric comes in various widths, the amount needed is given for up to three different fabric widths. Select the measurement appropriate to your clothes size and to the width of fabric that you have chosen.

LAYING OUT THE PATTERN

Where applicable, follow the cutting layout for the width of the fabric you have chosen. This appears at the beginning of a project. Each pattern piece is numbered so it can be easily identified on the cutting layouts (see page 148). Broken lines indicate the reverse side of the pattern pieces, so they should be placed with the right side facing down on the fabric. Where the lines of the pattern pieces in the cutting layouts are continuous, these should be placed right side up.

For double thickness, fold the fabric with right sides together and lay the pattern pieces on the wrong side. For single thickness, lay the pattern pieces on the right side of the fabric. When more than one of the same piece is to be cut one at a time, reverse the paper pattern for the second piece.

NAP

The nap is a pile produced by directional raised fibres on fabrics such as velvet. Fabrics with a pile or a one-way pattern must be cut with all the pattern pieces placed facing the same direction. The yardage (or meterage) required in this book is for fabrics without nap, so you should allow for extra if you choose a fabric with nap or a one-way design. When working with a nap, the pattern should be pinned to the wrong side of the fabric before cutting.

The direction of the pile can be found by brushing your hand over the material. Brushing with the direction of the nap will feel smooth, whereas brushing against the nap will feel rough. A shiny, silky look is produced when the nap is running down. When the nap is running up, the fabric shade is deeper and richer.

CUTTING OUT THE PATTERN PIECES

Pin the pattern pieces to the fabric so that the pins lay in the same direction and do not obstruct the cutting line. Use enough pins to hold the pattern down, taking care not to pucker the fabric. Using sharp scissors, place one hand flat on the pattern and fabric to hold it down, keeping it flat so the lines being cut are accurate. Cut away from you along the seam line – the solid lines of the pattern. Cut notches outwards, rather than in to the seam allowance.

Broken lines in the cutting layout indicate the reverse side of a pattern piece. Place the pattern with the right side facing down on the fabric.

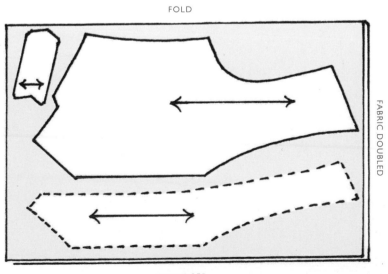

STITCHES

These essential hand and machine stitches are the foundations for sewing a beautifully tailored garment suitable for the discerning gentleman.

HAND STITCHES

Hand stitches are usually worked from right to left. To secure the end of the thread to the fabric, work a few stitches over each other at the beginning. Alternatively, knot the end of the thread and insert the needle from the wrong side of the fabric.

Tacking (basting) stitch

Tacking or basting is a temporary stitch used to join pieces of fabric ready for fitting and permanent stitching. It is the easiest and quickest hand-sewing stitch. Knot the end of the thread and work large stitches from right to left.

Finish with a couple of stitches worked over each other to secure the end. When the seam has been permanently sewn by machine or hand, remove the tacking stitches.

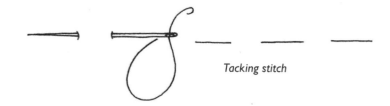

Tacking stitch

Slipstitch

This stitch produces an almost invisible finish, used for hemming and attaching trimmings. Pass the needle through the folded edge and, at the same point, pick up a thread or two of the fabric underneath. Continue in this way, spacing the stitches evenly around ⅛–¼in (0.3–0.6cm) apart.

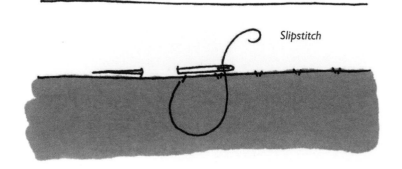

Slipstitch

Hem stitch

Bring the thread through to the edge of the folded hem. Pick up a thread of fabric and pass the needle diagonally through the edge of the hem. Continue in this way, spacing the stitches around ¼in (0.6cm) apart.

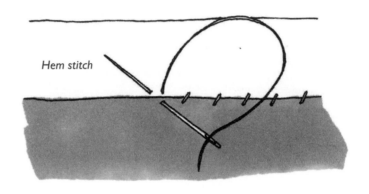

Hem stitch

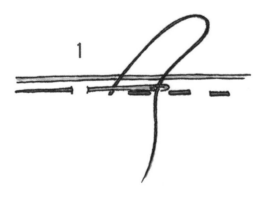

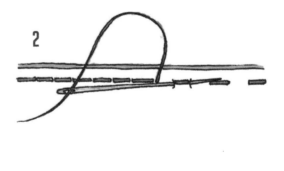

DOUBLE RUNNING STITCH

This stitch is used to join the seams of the slippers on page 104.

1 Sew a line of running stitches to join the pieces. Do not fasten off at the end.

2 Turn the work and sew in between the gaps of the stitches just worked.

MACHINE STITCHES

Staystitching

This is a straight machine stitch used around curved and angled edges, such as at necklines, to prevent stretching when handling before joining pieces together. The stitching is done ⅛in (0.3cm) inside the seam line. The stitches do not need to be removed because they will be hidden between the seam allowance and the edge inside the finished garment.

Zigzag stitch

The zigzag stitch is available on most sewing machines, although very old machines often only do straight stitching. Zigzag can be used as a decorative stitch with a contrasting thread, or for finishing raw edges. By adjusting the length and width of the stitch, zigzagging will make a neat buttonhole.

Topstitching

This is a line of straight machine stitching worked on the right side of the fabric, parallel to seams and edges. It is used as both a decorative and a functional stitch.

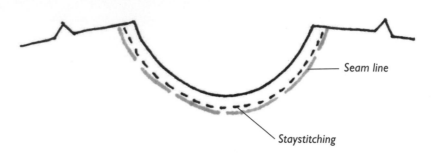

Seam line

Staystitching

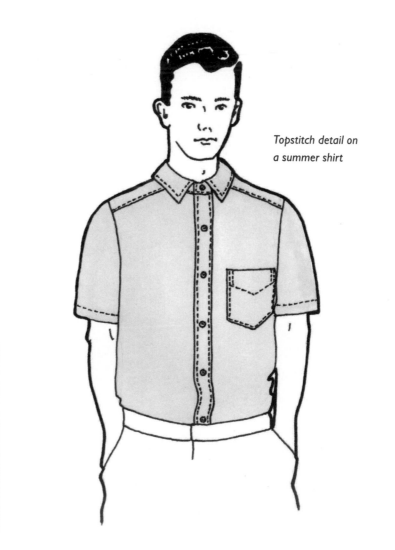

Topstitch detail on a summer shirt

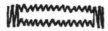

Zigzag stitch used for a buttonhole (above) and to finish a raw edge (right)

SEAMS

A seam is where two pieces of a garment are joined. The type of seam you use will depend on the fabric, design and finished look you wish to produce.

PINNING SEAMS

Pinning and tacking seams is very useful if you are a beginner, ensuring the fabric will not slip about when stitching, so producing a neat seam and avoiding mistakes. As your confidence builds with experience, you may feel you no longer need to pin seams before you stitch.

Pinning fabric along the seam line

Insert the pins so that the points face away from you. As the pins cannot be stitched over when in line with the needle, they will be easy to remove with the pinheads facing towards you; you will also avoid pricking your finger.

Stitching over pins

Pins can be machine stitched over when they are at right angles to the edge of the work. This way, the needle will not get broken by hitting the pins and the pins can be removed after stitching the seam. This is a particularly useful method when easing the fullness of fabric.

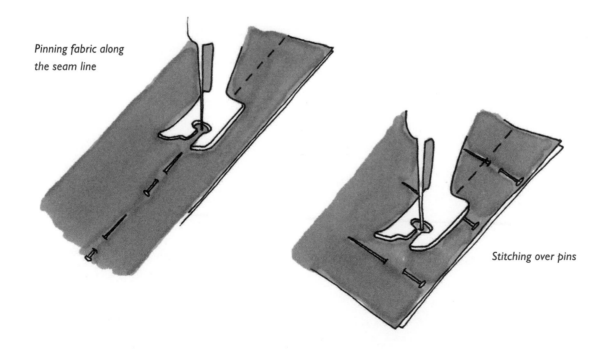

Pinning fabric along the seam line

Stitching over pins

FLAT SEAMS

The patterns in this book use a flat seam unless otherwise stated.

With right sides of fabric together, stitch along the ⅝in (1.5cm) seam line and press the seam open. To secure the line of stitching and prevent the stitches from unravelling, run the machine backwards and then forwards over the first and last few stitches. The raw edges of the seam can be trimmed to neaten it.

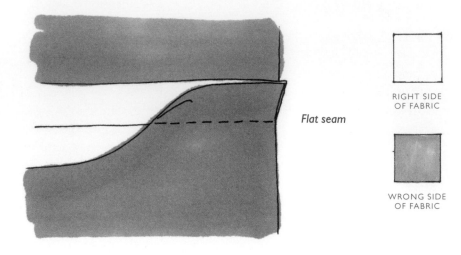

Flat seam

RIGHT SIDE
OF FABRIC

WRONG SIDE
OF FABRIC

CLIPPING SEAMS

Where a seam is shaped, snipping or cutting notches into the fabric will enable it to lie flat. On fabrics that fray easily, cut the layers of the seams separately and make sure the snips and notches of each seam do not match. To reduce bulk in heavier fabrics, seams can be layered so they lay flat by cutting each layer of the seam slightly smaller than the last.

Clipping curved seams

For seams that curve outwards, cut a V-shape into the seam close to the stitch line. For inward curves, snip a straight line in the seam close to the stitches.

Trimming corners

Corners should be trimmed to an angle so the fabric lies flat when the work is turned right side out. An inverted corner should be snipped close to the seam line.

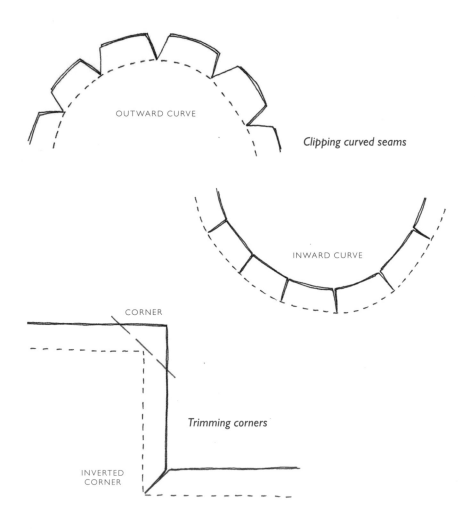

OUTWARD CURVE

Clipping curved seams

INWARD CURVE

CORNER

Trimming corners

INVERTED
CORNER

SEAM FINISHES

Finishing the seams will neaten the garment and prevent fraying, therefore making it more durable. All the seams in the projects in this book should be finished as they are stitched, by using any of the following methods:

Turned edge

Turn under the raw edges of the seam and stitch close to the fold.

Zigzag finish

Work a line of zigzag stitches close to the raw edges of the seam. Practise on a scrap of fabric beforehand to achieve the desired stitch length and width.

Bound edges

Press the seam open. If using purchased bias binding, one side will be slightly narrower than the other. With the narrow edge of the binding on the right side of the seam, wrap the binding around the raw edge. Stitch close to the edge of the binding.

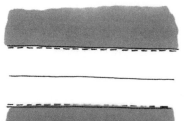

Turned edge

Zigzag finish

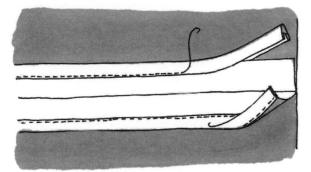

Bound edges

Hong Kong finish

Use 1in (2.5cm) wide bias strips or press open double-folded purchased bias binding.

1 Press the seam open. With right sides together, aligning the raw edges, pin the bias strip to the seam. Stitch together, allowing a ¼in (0.6cm) seam.

2 Turn the bias strip over the seam to the inside and press. On the right side of the seam, stitch inside the line of the previous stitches to catch the bottom edge of the binding and enclose the raw edge.

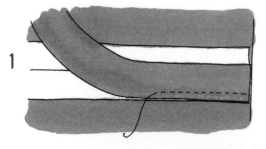

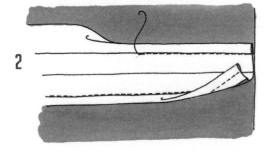

SPECIAL SEAMS

The raw edges of the following seams do not need any finishing. These seams are both neat and will withstand the rigours of regular laundering.

French seam

Where the pattern states that the right sides of the fabric should be together to sew the seam, start a French seam with the wrong sides of the fabric together.

1 Stitch the first seam with wrong sides together, working ¼in (0.6cm) from the raw edge.

2 Trim the seam. Press the seam to one side, then turn the work to the inside and press.

3 With right sides together, stitch along the seam allowance to encase the first seam.

When a French seam is stitched on a curved line, snip the first seam to allow it to expand around the curve so that it sits flat inside the second line of stitches.

French seam

Flat-fell seam

The stitching forms a decorative seam that is visible on the right side of the fabric. It is used for lingerie but is also suitable for heavier garments, such as jeans and outerwear. Where the seam is curved, a French seam is more suitable.

1 With wrong sides of fabric together, stitch along the ⅝in (1.5cm) seam line and press it to one side.

2 Trim the lower edge seam allowance to ⅛in (0.3cm). Turn under and press ¼in (0.6m) on the raw edge of the other seam allowance.

3 Press the wider seam allowance over the narrow, trimmed edge and stitch down, close to the fold, encasing the raw edge.

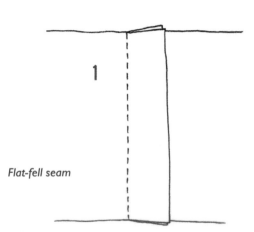

Flat-fell seam

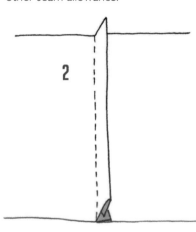

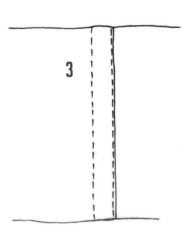

DARTS

Darts create shaping by controlling the fullness in fabric to fit the garment smoothly over the contours of the body.

1 Before removing the paper pattern from the cut-out fabric piece, make small holes in the pattern paper at the pointed end and along the lines of the dart. Mark the position of the dart on the fabric with a tailor's chalk pencil.

2 With right sides together, fold the centre of the dart, matching the lines on each side. Stitch carefully from the wide end, tapering off to the point. Vertical darts should be pressed towards the centre front or centre back; horizontal darts should be pressed towards the hem of the garment.

3 To reduce bulk in heavy-weight fabric, slash to within ½in (1.25cm) of the point of the dart and press open.

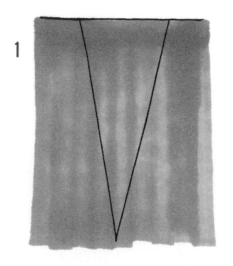

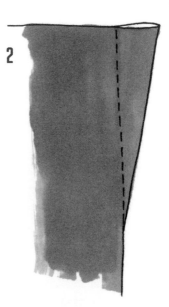

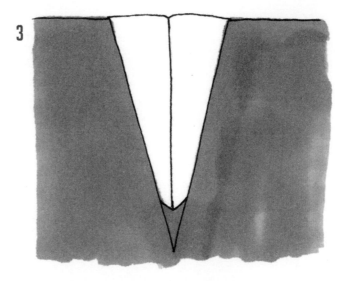

   RIGHT SIDE OF FABRIC

   WRONG SIDE OF FABRIC

GATHERING

Gathering is a simple method to adjust fullness in the fabric and to ease seams, such as on the head of a sleeve.

GATHERING BY HAND OR MACHINE

Straight rows of running stitches are used to gather fabric by hand. Tacking thread can be used, as the stitches are temporary and will be removed after the seam is permanently stitched. A straight stitch is used for gathering by machine. The sewing machine should be set to the longest stitch, so that the stitches are easy to gather and remove later.

1 Sew along the seam line of the section to be gathered, leaving a free length of thread at each end. Work another row of stitches ¼in (0.6cm) inside the seam allowance.

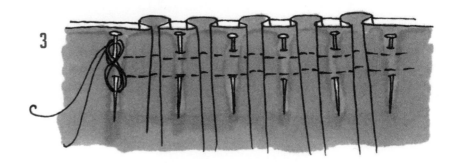

2 Pull a thread from each row at the same time to gather one half of the section. Insert a pin in the fabric and secure the threads by winding them in a figure of eight around it. Repeat for the other side to fit the required measurement.

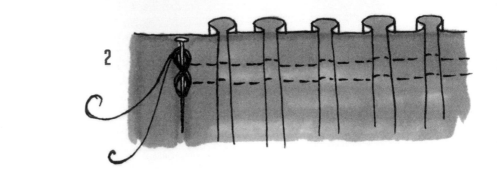

3 Pin the gathered edge to the piece to be joined, matching notches, any seams and relevant markings. Adjust the gathers so that they are distributed evenly between the pins. Remove the gathering stitches only after the seams have been permanently stitched.

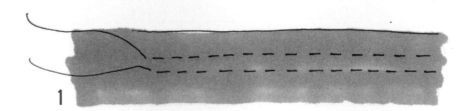

HEMS

Choose which hem finish to use depending on the style of the garment and on the weight of the cloth and whether it is prone to fraying.

Stitched and turned hem

This method is suitable for fabrics that do not fray easily. Turn under the hem allowance and tack in place, close to the fold of the hem. Turn under and press ¼in (0.6cm) on the raw edge. Stitch close to the fold. Slipstitch (see page 154) the hem in place, just under the fold.

Bound hem

This method is suitable for fabrics that fray. Turn under the hem allowance and tack in place, close to the fold of the hem. Open out one edge of a strip of bias binding and, with right sides together, stitch to the raw edge of the hem. Turn up the hem and slipstitch (see page 154) the folded top edge of the bias binding to the inside of the garment.

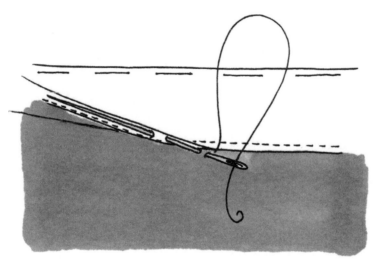

Stitched and turned hem

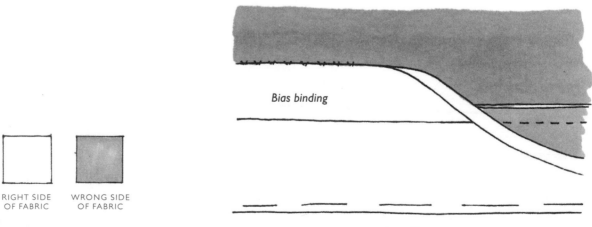

Bias binding

Bound hem

RIGHT SIDE OF FABRIC	WRONG SIDE OF FABRIC

PRESSING

Equipment used for pressing is just as important as the sewing tools. The finished appearance of a project will benefit from carefully pressing each seam, pleat and dart as you stitch them.

PRESSING EQUIPMENT

Have all the equipment for pressing close to hand and set up ready to use as you sew. Remove all pins and tacking stitches before pressing.

Iron

The iron should have adjustable heat settings for different fibres and a choice of steam or heat only. Steam produces the right amount of moisture to set a collar or lapel and will create a crisp edge and flat seam. Use the point of the iron to open seams. Use a dry cloth if applying the iron directly to the fabric. If the iron is being held away from the fabric when steaming, a cloth is not required.

Ironing board

The ironing board should be well padded and sturdy. Set it up at a height at which you are comfortable standing.

Tailor's ham

This is a shaped cushion that is firmly stuffed and ideal for pressing curved areas and darts.

Pressing cloth

Press on the wrong side using a damp or dry cloth, if necessary, to protect the fabric from the heat of the iron and prevent shine. Muslin makes a good pressing cloth since it is see-through; it can be used in a single layer or folded to adapt to the weight of the material you are pressing.

Sleeve board

A sleeve board is useful for pressing sleeve seams and other places that will not fit on the ironing board.

Seam roll

This is a long fabric-covered roll that is used for pressing seams.

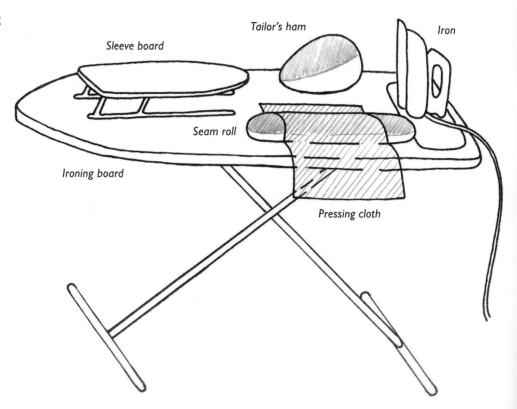

Sleeve board

Tailor's ham

Iron

Seam roll

Ironing board

Pressing cloth

HOW TO MAKE A TAILOR'S HAM

1 Cut an oval-shaped pattern from paper measuring around 9 × 12in (23 × 30cm). From the pattern, cut two oval shapes in a firm calico, cotton or wool.

2 With right sides together, stitch around the outside edge, allowing a seam of ⅝in (1.5cm) and leaving an opening. Work a second line of stitching close to the first to reinforce the seam. Trim the seams and notch the curves.

3 Turn right sides out. Stuff very firmly with fine sawdust. Toy stuffing will not be firm enough. Pour the sawdust through a cone rolled from paper or thin card.

4 Turn in the raw edges and hand stitch the opening together with strong, doubled thread.

PRESSING FABRICS

Pressing is not the same as ironing. The iron is set down onto the fabric and then lifted, rather than pulled across the fabric. Set the iron to the right temperature for the fabric and test on a scrap first.

Cotton
A hot iron over a damp cloth will remove any creases.

Linen
Press with a hot iron on the wrong side of the fabric.

Silk
Press with a medium heat, using a dry cloth to avoid the seam line marking the right side of the fabric. Using a damp cloth may cause water marks.

Synthetics
Use a cool iron, avoiding going over the seams as this can mark the fabric. Do not dampen the material, but pass a steam iron over the fabric without touching it with the iron.

Wool
Use a warm iron and damp cloth. Leave on the board to dry naturally.

Velvet
Fabric with a pile should not be pressed directly. Press as little as possible and only on the back of the fabric, placing the pile side down on a needle board or onto the pile side of an oddment of velvet. Velvet can be steamed, taking care not to get the fabric wet. Stand the iron upright and cover it with a damp cloth. Gently pass the velvet in front of the steam it produces to steam out any wrinkles.

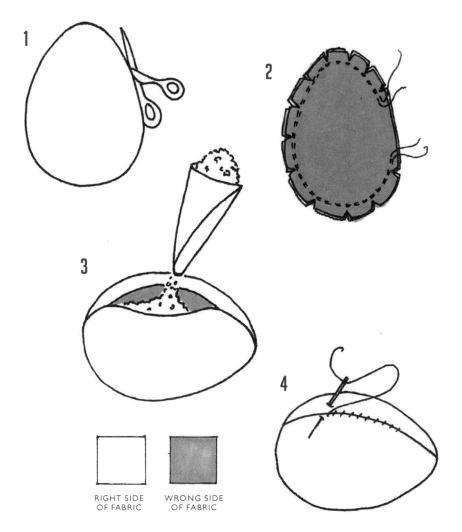

RIGHT SIDE OF FABRIC   WRONG SIDE OF FABRIC

FINISHING TOUCHES

The neatly bound edges, fastenings and their application are the details that will make your handmade project stand out as a one-of-a-kind piece.

Bias binding

Bias binding provides a neat finish as well as strengthening and concealing raw edges. It is widely available to buy with ready-pressed edges, making it simple to apply. However, it is easy to make using your own choice of fabric.

1 Find the bias of the fabric by folding it diagonally at one end. Mark the fabric with diagonal lines, parallel to the bias fold. The lines should be the desired width of your binding with an extra ¼in (0.6cm) each side for the seams.

2 The short ends, which are cut on the grain, will be diagonal. With right sides together, pin and stitch the short ends together and press the seam open.

3 Fold both long edges in to the centre and press.

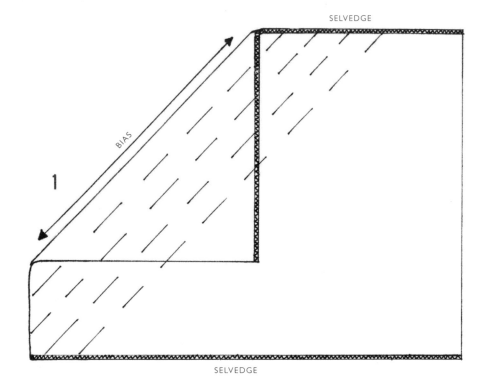

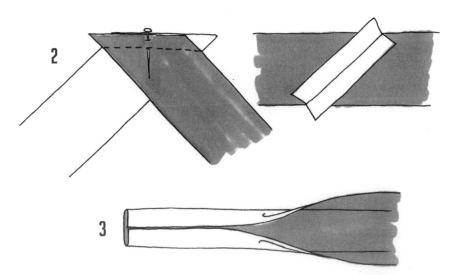

Binding outward corners

1 Open out one of the pressed edges of the binding and, with right side of binding to the wrong side of the garment, pin in place. Stitch along the seam to the corner, stopping at the seam line. Run the machine back and forth over a few stitches to reinforce the seam.

2 Fold the binding around the corner, aligning the fold with the edge just stitched. Pin and stitch the binding right along the adjoining edge of the corner. This will create a mitred edge on the right side of the binding.

3 Turn the binding to the right side of the garment, folding it at the corner so the mitre faces the opposite direction from the one on the inside. Pin over the seams and slipstitch (see page 154) by hand or topstitch (see page 156) in place close to the edges, pivoting the needle at the corners. The mitre at each corner can also be slipstitched.

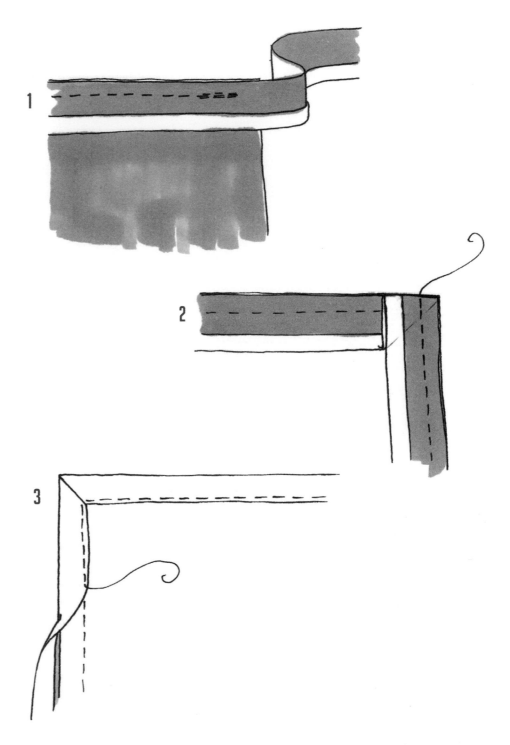

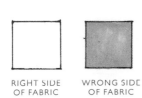

RIGHT SIDE
OF FABRIC

WRONG SIDE
OF FABRIC

BUTTONHOLES

Many of the projects in this book are fastened with buttons. The machine-worked buttonhole is a quick and easy method. Hand-stitched buttonholes take longer, but produce a beautiful finish to a garment.

Machine-worked buttonhole

Modern machines often have an automatic buttonhole attachment. However, a neat buttonhole can be produced using zigzag stitch. This buttonhole is worked when the facings are already attached. Mark the position of the buttonholes. Take care to keep the lines straight and the stitches close together. At each end, the stitches should be wider than those down each side of the length. Cut the opening after stitching using buttonhole scissors.

Machine-worked buttonhole

Hand-worked buttonhole

Mark the position of the buttonholes before you start. Make sure your stitches are even and close together.

1 Work a row of stitches by machine ⅛in (0.3cm) on each side and across both ends of the buttonhole marking. Carefully cut the length of the buttonhole with sharp scissors.

2 With the right side of the work facing, stitch around the edges by inserting the needle through the cut line and out just beyond the line of stitching. Keep the thread under the point of the needle and draw the needle up to tighten the thread, forming a little knot at the cut edge. Keep the stitches evenly spaced and equal in length.

3 Fan the stitches around the end towards the opening of the garment and work a straight bar of stitches at the other end to prevent the buttonhole from splitting.

Hand-worked buttonhole

1

2

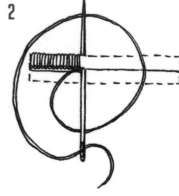

3

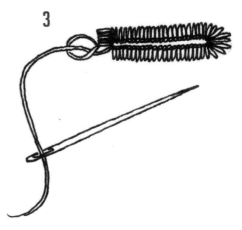

BUTTONS

Many buttons have a shank (a raised part underneath), allowing room for the thickness of the fabric around the buttonhole. Buttons without a shank need to be attached in such a way as to form a shank with the thread, so that it is easy to fasten and sit neatly on the fabric. Use thread coated with beeswax (see page 140) to sew the buttons to the garment.

1 Mark the position of the button on the fabric. For horizontal buttonholes, the position of the shank should be near the end closest to the opening. For vertical buttonholes, the shank should be central.

2 Secure the thread to the fabric. Place a matchstick or hairgrip over the button and work over it when sewing the button. When the button feels secure, remove the matchstick or hairgrip.

3 Pull the needle through so that the thread lies between the button and the fabric. Slide the button to the top of the stitches and wind the thread around the stitches under the button to form a shank. Work some stitches through the shank and fasten off securely on the wrong side of the fabric.

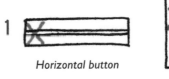

Horizontal button

Vertical button

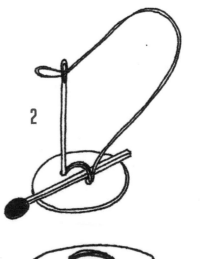

BAR TACK

Bar tacks are worked on the right side of the garment to reinforce the ends of pockets, seams and pleats. When stitched by hand, use embroidery or buttonhole thread.

By machine

Work a line of straight stitches to mark the position and length of the bar tack. Change the machine setting to a zigzag stitch, keeping the stitches very narrow and short. Zigzag over the straight stitches to complete the bar tack.

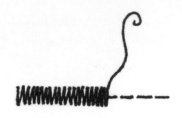

Bar tack by machine

By hand

1 Work a few long stitches through the fabric across the ends of the opening.

2 Cover the long stitches with short, straight stitches, sewing them close together and picking up a few threads of the fabric at the same time.

3 To finish the ends of the bar tack, work small bar tacks at right angles to it.

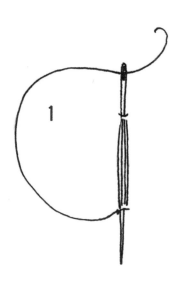
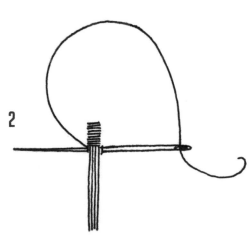
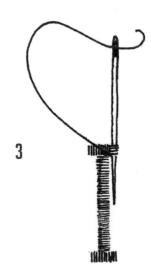

Bar tack by hand

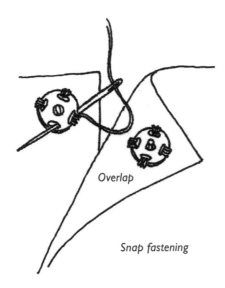

Overlap

Snap fastening

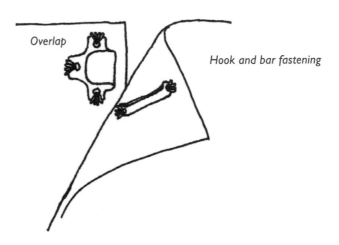

Overlap

Hook and bar fastening

SNAP FASTENING/MAGNETIC SEW-ON CLASP

Stitch the ball half of the snap fastening or magnetic clasp to the underside of the overlap, working several small stitches over each other through each hole. Carry the thread from one hole to the next, under the snap. To mark the position of the socket half, rub tailor's chalk onto the ball of the snap and place against the fabric where it will be fastened. Stitch the socket half of the snap or magnetic clasp in position.

HOOK AND BAR FASTENING

Sew the hook to the inside of the opening edge, working several small stitches over each other through each hole. Take care that the stitches don't show on the right side of the garment. Stitch the bar to the outside of the garment, on the underlap. The bar should come just under the bend of the hook when the garment is lapped.

ABBREVIATIONS

cm	centimetres
m	metres
mm	millimetres
yd	yards

RESOURCES

FABRIC AND FELT

FRANCE

Lil Weasel
1 Passage du Grand Cerf
75002 Paris
Tel: +33 (0)17 371 7048
www.lilweasel.fr

UK

Blooming Felt Ltd
Unit 27
Chamberlains Farm
Sporhams Lane
Danbury
Essex
CM3 4AJ
Tel: +44 (0)1245 471690
www.bloomingfelt.co.uk

Cloth House
47 Berwick Street
London
W1F 8SJ
Tel: +44 (0)20 7437 5155
47@clothhouse.com
www.clothhouse.com

Ditto Fabrics
21 Kensington Gardens
Brighton
East Sussex
BN1 4AL
Tel: +44 (0)1273 603771
sales@dittofabrics.co.uk
www.dittofabrics.co.uk

MacCulloch and Wallis
25–26 Poland Street
London W1F 8QN
Tel: +44 (0)20 7629 0311
samples@macculloch.com
www.macculloch-wallis.co.uk

Merchant & Mills Limited
14A Tower Street
Rye
East Sussex
TN31 7AT
Tel: +44 (0)1797 227789
www.merchantandmills.com

The Stitchery
12–16 Riverside
Cliffe Bridge
High Street
Lewes
East Sussex
BN7 2RE
Tel: +44 (0)1273 473577
info@the-stitchery.co.uk
www.the-stitchery.co.uk

Wayward
68 Norman Road
St. Leonards-on-Sea
East Sussex
TN38 0EJ
Tel: +44 (0)78 1501 3337
info@wayward.co
www.wayward.co

USA

Brooklyn General Store
128 Union St
Brooklyn
New York 11231
Tel: +1 718 237 7753
www.brooklyngeneral.com

Habu Textiles
Tel: +1 888 667 4030
habu@habutextiles.com
www.habutextiles.com

Purl Soho
459 Broome Street
New York 10013
Tel: +1 212 420 8796
www.purlsoho.com

The Felt Pod
Tel: +1 818 809 2238
customerservice@thefeltpod.com
www.thefeltpod.com

SEWING TOOLS AND HABERDASHERY

FRANCE
Lil Weasel
(see Fabric and Felt)

Maison Sajou
47, rue du Caire
75002 Paris
Tel: +33 01 4233 4266
www.sajou.fr

UK
Ernest Wright and Son Limited
Endeavour Works
58 Broad Lane
Sheffield
S1 4BT
Tel: +44 (0)1142 754812
www.ernestwright.co.uk

MacCulloch and Wallis
(see Fabric and Felt)

Merchant & Mills Limited
(see Fabric and Felt)

The Swagman's Daughter
www.theswagmansdaughter.com

Tailor Mouse Limited
27 Carr Beck Drive
Castleford
West Yorkshire
WF10 5TH
Tel: +44 (0)1423 819425
www.tailormouse.co.uk

The Stitchery
(see Fabric and Felt)

Wayward
(see Fabric and Felt)

USA
Brooklyn General Store
(see Fabric and Felt)

Habu Textiles
(see Fabric and Felt)

Purl Soho
(see Fabric and Felt)

ACKNOWLEDGEMENTS

Author's acknowledgements: I would like to thank Jonathan Bailey very much for giving me the opportunity to write *The Gentleman's Wardrobe*. Thank you to Wendy McAngus for all her support and patience, and thank you to everyone at GMC. I wish to thank my daughters Miriam, Dilys and Honey, who have been very encouraging, and thank you to my granddaughters, Dolly and Winter, for their interest and enthusiasm in what I do. I would like to dedicate this book to my husband Damian and my son Flynn, who patiently tried on toiles so I could make adjustments to the patterns, and who answered my endless questions about the projects I was working on. Finally, a special dedication goes to my grandson Leo, the youngest gentleman in the family, for whom I shall look forward to making miniature versions of these projects.

GMC Publications would like to thank: Marcus from Zone Model Agency; Chris Gloag and Richard Boll for photography, assisted by Guillaume Serve; Jen Dodson for her marvellous hair and make up; The Green Door Store, Brighton and Paul Clark Clothiers, Lewes for allowing us to photograph there; Ben Mothersole, Ben Nolan, Matthew Oldfield, Jude Rose and Rob Trueman for lending costumes and props. Label on pages 10-25: Shutterstock/NataLT.

INDEX

To order a book,
or to request a catalogue,
contact: GMC Publications Ltd,
166 High Street, Lewes,
East Sussex, BN7 1XU,
United Kingdom

Tel: +44 (0)1273 488005
www.gmcbooks.com